The Autobiography of
St. John Neumann, C.SS.R.

With
Introduction, Translation,
Commentary and Epilogue
by
Alfred C. Rush, C.SS.R.

Foreword by
His Eminence, John Cardinal Krol

Pauline
BOOKS & MEDIA
Boston

Imprimi Potest:

Joseph L. Kerins, C.SS.R.
Provincial, Baltimore Province

Nihil Obstat:

Francis M. Salmon, C.SS.R.
Censor Deputatus

Imprimatur:

+William Cardinal Baum,
Archbishop of Washington

December 16, 1976

Library of Congress Cataloging-in-Publication Data

Neumann, John Nepomucene, Bp., 1811-1860.
The autobiography of St. John Neumann, C.SS.R., fourth
bishop of Philadelphia.

ISBN 0-8198-0384-7

Includes index.
1. Neumann. John Nepomucene, Bp., 1811-1860.
2. Catholic Church—Bishops—Biography. 3. Bishops—
Pennsylvania—Philadelphia—Biography. 4. Philadelphia—
Biography. I. Rush, Alfred Clement, 1910-
BX4705.N45A32   282'.092'4 [B]   77-5317

Photos courtesy of Neumann Center, Philadelphia, PA

Printed and published in the U.S.A. by Pauline Books & Media,
50 Saint Pauls Avenue, Boston MA 02130-3491.

www.pauline.org

Pauline Books & Media is the publishing house of the Daughters
of St. Paul, an international congregation of women religious
serving the Church with the communications media.

2 3 4 5 6 7 8   05 04 03 02 01 00

Contents

Foreword

Through his diligent work Father Alfred C. Rush, C.SS.R., presents us with the life of John Nepomucene Neumann, my predecessor in Philadelphia, as that saintly man himself wrote it. Father Rush adds informative comment when necessary and completes the story of the bishop's life in the epilogue.

In this Foreword it would be superfluous to give a précis of the life of John Nepomucene Neumann. Let his own words speak for themselves. However, it is altogether fitting to recall certain facts about which many may not be aware.

The future saint came to the United States from Middle Europe at a time when few of the Catholics of the United States came from that region. He was born a citizen of the Austro-Hungarian Empire which was made up of many nations, Although his name was German, the bishop considered himself a Bohemian, a Czech, and Czech was his native tongue, but in boyhood he learned German, the second of six modern languages in which he was to become proficient. In view of possible service in North America he had learned English and French in Prague; after arrival in the United States he learned Gaelic and Italian to serve better other fellow immigrants.

It was altogether fitting that in his See-city the Forty-first Eucharistic Congress was celebrated in the year which would see the approval of his future canonization because Bishop Neumann was the one to introduce to the United States the celebration of the Forty Hours, that special devotion to the Holy Eucharist which is the annual occasion for manifesting special devotion to Jesus in the Eucharist.

His concern for Catholic education is well known. He is called the father of the parochial school; he was the first bishop to strive to establish a school in each parish of his diocese and during his apostolate in the Church in Philadelphia, which at that time embraced the Eastern half of Pennsylvania plus West Jersey (which we in good part know as South Jersey) and Delaware, the number of students in Catholic schools increased twenty fold.

His, by our standards, was not a long life. He lived less than fifty years. But his accomplishments were great and his vision even greater.

On the occasion of his beatification Pope Paul VI said of Bishop Neumann, "Neumann was a pioneer; he was in a certain sense a founder; he was one of that marvelous chain of bishops which prepared the cadres of the Catholic hierarchy in the United States and infused into it those virtues of dedication, of zeal, of efficient practicality, of absolute fidelity, which distinguish now the venerable and exemplary American Episcopate." The life of John Neumann remains a challenge to all of us, not only bishops but also all Catholics of the United States, to manifest to all the world our loyalty to Jesus Christ and His Church.

John Cardinal Krol
Archbishop of Philadelphia
December 22, 1976

Introduction

The headquarters and archives of the Redemptorists' Baltimore Province are now located in Brooklyn, N.Y.[1] These archives contain a manuscript, entitled, *Kurze Lebensbeschreib ung des P. Joh. Nep. Neumann, Priesters der Versammlung des hl. Erlösers und erwählten Bischofs von Philadelphia in Nord-America.* The English translation reads: *A Short Account of the Life of Father John Nep. Neumann of the Congregation of the Most Holy Redeemer, and Bishop-Elect of Philadelphia in North America.* The essential data on this manuscript is contained in the opening words and in the date at the end. The manuscript is dated March 27, 1852. This was the eve of Neumann's ordination as bishop. The opening words are *Ex obedientia,* that is, *Under obedience.* The order to write this account of his life came to Neumann from Father Bernard Hafkenscheid, C.SS.R., who was the first one to hold the office of Provincial after the foundations in the United States, that go back to 1832, were constituted as an independent Province on June 29, 1850.[2] Historians will gladly leave to the canonists the discussion whether a Provincial can give a Bishop-Elect a command of obedience. They will rejoice in having such a valuable Neumann manuscript. The thought of having a Neumann autobiography is typical of Father Hafkenscheid, the celebrated missionary from Holland, the very capable Provincial, who showed himself a man of big ideas and wide vision.[3]

The manuscript is made up of four folios, each measuring $9^{7/8"}$ x $7^{5/8"}$. Neumann numbered them 1-4. In other words, he did not number the verso side of each page or folio. The short autobiography takes up three and a half pages or seven sides. It seems surprising at first that such a manuscript amounts to twenty pages in Father Sampers' printed edition.[4] However, this element of surprise completely vanishes when one learns more about the handwriting and other features of the manuscript.

The manuscript is written in the German or Gothic script. It has all the characteristics of Neumann's handwriting, that is, very small letters written very closely together. The space between the letters, the words and the lines is very close and crammed. Some letters are not completely formed. At times the last parts of many words are not spelled out completely, but merely indicated. Also, Neumann makes frequent use of abbreviations. These are either standard or easily understood German abbreviations. A German edition could well take note of these points; there is no need of this in an English translation. One also notes that many names of persons or places are given their phonetic spelling and are not the proper orthographic spelling, e.g., Chakert for Czackert, Milwauky for Milwaukee. Without calling attention to each instance, the translation gives the proper spelling.

This autobiography was written from memory. This accounts for some chronological mistakes, which the translation notes. Besides being written from memory, it also had to be written somewhat hastily. One notes corrections that Neumann himself introduced, e.g., by adding, dropping or changing a word, phrase or date. The German edition rightly notes such corrections; the English translation needs only to give the corrected version. Occasionally, a word is repeated twice. A much more important problem arises when a word or phrase is lacking in the manuscript. In the interests of intelligibility, Father Sampers makes a probable conjecture and adds a word or phrase. These are enclosed in brackets. Brackets are also used in the German text to indicate a correction of a German construction, e.g., kann for konnte. A question mark enclosed in brackets indicates the best possible interpretation of a difficult reading.[5]

Neumann scholars owe a great debt of gratitude to Father Andreas Sampers for his critical edition and scrupulously-exact transliteration of the manuscript. As is very evident from what has been said up to the present, the transliteration of the German from handwriting to print is beset with difficulties. Specialist that he is in manuscripts, Father Sampers speaks of the great work involved with this manuscript; he also speaks of the help from experts whom he consulted.[6] This present work is based on the Neumann manuscript and the Sampers' edition. This offers an occasion to pay well-deserved compliment to Father Sampers' edition and to say that this work would not have been done without his help, especially his transliteration. It is relatively easy to go from the printed text to the manuscript handwriting. The reverse is a completely different story, especially when one looks at the script and the handwriting of this manuscript.

The transliteration of a text leads to its translation. This brings up more problems because translation has problems all its own. The basic problem is to take a German manuscript of 1852 and make it an English document of 1977. Hardly is the translator into his work than he finds that German has a logic and psychology all its own in contrast to the logic and psychology of English. This is further complicated by the logic and psychology of the original author and his translator. The translation is from German to English. The aim has been to be true to the German and have the finished product read like English. In this process, one cannot be slavish and translate word for word; rather, there must be freedom to translate from sense to sense and meaning to meaning. In this sphere, one can apply the Gospel-saying about the letter that kills and the spirit that gives life.

Coming down to specifics, this English translation had to break up some of the long, involved, cumbersome German sentences. To link the sentences together, an occasional word or phrase had to be inserted; this is indicated by the use of brackets. Brackets are also used by the translator to indicate an event by the month and the day where the original indicates it only by a liturgical feast. German uses the phrase "Rev. Mr." to refer to a diocesan priest and "Rev. Father" to designate a priest of a religious order; English calls for the simple title, Father, for both. There is a certain stiffness and proper formalism in Neumann's use of titles that hardly lends itself to the English ear and practice. Neumann says, e.g., "The Reverend Bishop of New York, Dr. Dubois;" this becomes "Bishop Dubois of New York."

Even if the translation were crystal clear, the reader could still experience some difficulty in understanding certain episodes. This is because Neumann often compresses so much of life into a few lines. Also, he is often speaking of an event as lived through and finished. The reader, therefore, must learn to read in the perspective of Neumann. On page 25, the sentence that begins: "At the end of the [school] year, 1827," is the first of only two sentences that deal with his educational crisis in the final year of what we would call High School. He was tempted to give up, but he let himself be talked into going back by his mother and sister, Veronica. Obviously, one thinks that the next sentence is going to be about going back. In a way, it is. However, Neumann is writing about this in the perspective of 1852. He speaks of the last two years of that period of education as already completed, a happy period in which he enjoyed the Humanities under a good teacher. The closer Neumann comes to the end of the autobiography, so much more does this compressed quality appear. This is true of his Redemptorist years. It almost takes a Redemptorist, a specialist in the history of those early days, to follow him intelligently. Episodes like this call for notes in the interests of clarity and intelligibility.

Notes are called for. In giving notes, the books and sources to be used will be clear. However, there are other Neumann archival sources that should be introduced here. The first is Neumann's Journal (*Mon Journal*). This was begun in 1834 and was continued almost until he became a Redemptorist novice in 1840. Not so much a diary, but an examination of conscience, the entries in it are mostly in French and German.[7] Attention should also be directed to the Rodler Papers (RP). These are the letters that Neumann wrote to his relatives and priest friends back home. They were (1952) in Budweis Diocesan Archives; copies of them are in RABB.[8] The Berger Papers (BP) are the material collected by John Berger, C.SS.R., the bishop's nephew, when he began to gather material for his uncle's biography, beginning in 1872.[9] In this way there came into being the first biography of Bishop Neumann that appeared in German in 1883 and in English translation the following year.[10]

From some of the things mentioned above, it is clear that this autobiography is not without defects. Furthermore, its brevity constitutes a drawback. Despite this, the autobiography is an important document. Here one can begin with the manuscript itself. It is known that Neumann wrote this, *currente calamo*, that he was hurried and meeting a deadline. Despite this, the general appearance of the manuscript is orderly. By no means can it be described as careless. Even though he was meeting a deadline, his manuscript shows a non-hurried soul, a non-pressured soul, a person who had the situation under control.[11]

When we turn from the manuscript to the material, we find important Neumann information. Here it will be helpful to show, quantitatively, how many pages are devoted to the various episodes of Neumann's life. This will be based on the writer's typewritten manuscript. Four pages (1-4) trace Neumann's childhood until his completion of grammar school (1811-1823). Five pages cover the course of his education, beginning with the Budweis *Gymnasium* through the end of the fourth year of theology at the University of Prague (1823-1835). Seven pages (10-17) are taken up with his plans to do missionary work in America, his travelings across Europe from Prachatitz to Havre, his voyage across the Atlantic to New York (1835-1836). Five pages (17-22) treat his years as a diocesan priest of New York (1836-1840). In four pages (22-26) he describes his odyssey as a Redemptorist novice (1840-1842). Not quite two pages (26-28) covers his Redemptorist life up to the eve of his episcopal ordination (1842-1852).

To have all this material is a blessing; to have it in autobiographical form is a double blessing. The autobiography is also important because it furnishes us with material that is hard to come by or that we would never know unless Neumann himself told us. The autobiography takes us into the intimacy of his home life and furnishes anecdotes that come from the family heart and hearth. Historians will be grateful for the details of his long years of education, of his itinerary across Europe on his way to America, and of his journeyings of what must be one of the most unique novitiates in the history of religious life. The autobiography is important for its account of Neumann's zeal as a diocesan priest of New York. Too often, in the popular mind, Neumann is thought of only as a Redemptorist or as a bishop. There is a tendency to forget that he was once a diocesan priest of New York. Rome, however, never forgets this period in its documents on Neumann as it points out how large a role these years played in the growth of his heroic holiness.[12]

The autobiography is even more important for the insight it gives us into the character of Neumann, into Neumann as a person. Here one thinks of the interpersonal relations of Neumann from the warmth of his home life through the friendships of his years of study and his work in the priesthood. In a special way the autobiography shows us how he faced life, how he coped with difficulties, disappointments and setbacks. An introduction is not meant to anticipate a story and rob the reader of learning it on his own. As the reader will see, hardly had Neumann emerged from the happy home life of grammar school days, when difficulties, disappointments and anxieties were part and parcel of each succeeding phase of his life. His difficulties in his many years of education culminated in having priests, University professors, who were more State-minded than Church-minded. It was a bitter disappointment to study for the priesthood only to find that there were to be no ordinations that year in the diocese of Budweis for the class of 1835. To leave for America without being able to give his parents the joy of seeing their son a priest was a sorrowful episode in his life. He had many an anxious hour when he was trying to get an American bishop to accept him for missionary work, and when he crossed the Atlantic not knowing whether he would find one after he had traveled close to two thousand miles. The four lonely years in his country parishes in the vicinity of Buffalo tell a story of heroic zeal. Heroic also is the only word to describe his perseverance as a Redemptorist novice when he saw himself sent, often so abruptly, to every Redemptorist foundation from Ohio to New York and Baltimore in the course of a single year, a year of Novitiate!

The autobiography, short as it is, helps us to understand why his cause was introduced at Rome,[13] why his virtue has been declared heroic,[14] and why he has already been beatified.[15] It also helps us to understand why the Second Vatican Council singles out Bishop Neumann when it wants to illustrate heroic holiness and when it wants to teach the balanced, consoling and encouraging doctrine about the possibility of heroic holiness in the call to holiness that applies to every follower of Christ.[16]

There now remains the pleasant task of rendering due thanks. I think of my Redemptorist confreres: Brother Barnabas Hipkins, the Provincial Archivist, who was so helpful with the manuscripts in the archives; Father Francis Salmon, our Rector here at Holy Redeemer, and Father Joseph Freund for their help in proofreading; Father Edward Droesch for the gigantic help he gave by his typing; Father Charles Fehrenbach, Ph.D., who read the translation, compared it word for word with the German and offered helpful corrections and suggestions; Father John Duffy, Ph.D., who read the translation and suggested stylistic improvements.

I also want to thank the Very Reverend Johannes Quasten, my colleague at the Catholic University of America, and the Reverend John Fuellenbach, S.V.D., a doctoral student in the department of Theology, for help in coming to the right understanding and meaning of some German words and phrases. I was fortunate to have so close at hand two whose mother tongue is German. Remaining in the University confines, I want to thank Miss Carolyn Lee, Mr. David Gilson, and Mrs. Shirley Pototsky of the Theology Divisional Library for their constant help. My thanks also go to Miss Virginia Murphy, Secretary to the Director of Libraries, for her generous help in typing. For the introduction to the Library of the National Geographic Society and the constant courtesies every time I worked there, I want to express my thanks to Mrs. Virginia Carter Hills and her staff. Lastly, I want to express warm thanks to my Provincial, the Very Reverend Joseph L. Kerins, C.SS.R., and his Consultors, the Very Reverends Joseph T. Hurley, C.SS.R., and Joseph F. Hart, C.SS.R., for their constant interest, help and encouragement.

Short Account of the Life of Father John Nepomucene Neumann, Priest of the Congregation of the Most Holy Redeemer and Bishop-Elect of Philadelphia in North America.

My parents, Philip Neumann[2] from Obernburg in Lower Franconia, Bavaria,[3] and Agnes[4] (nee Lebiš) had six children. The two oldest, Catherine[5] and Veronica,[6] both married widowers. I was the third child, born on Good Friday in the year of our Lord, 1811,[7] and baptized the same day in the town church of St. James the Greater. My godfather, John Marek,[8] mayor of the town, named me John Nepomucene, in honor of the glorious Patron of Bohemia.[9] The fourth child is my sister Joan, who entered the Sisters of St. Charles[10] in Prague after I left for America. She was the first novice to join the Order after it was brought here from Nancy in Lorraine. Known as Sister Caroline,[11] she is at present superior of the hospital in Budweis. The next to the youngest, my sister Louise, is still at home taking care of our aged father who, since the death of our mother three or four years ago, could not manage the large household alone. Furthermore, she has already [arranged for] living accommodations with the Sisters of St. Charles and will undoubtedly pursue her holy vocation as soon as her parental duty allows.[12] The youngest of us, Brother Wenceslaus, learned our father's trade of stocking weaving; later he followed me to America.[13]

Since I came to America, besides my mother, my sister Veronica has died and also the husband of my sister Catherine. Since Catherine, along with her son,[14] has a goodly income, we (the other brothers and sisters) agreed to give up our inheritance in favor of our father while he was living, and after his death for a hospital for the town of Prachatitz. Because of its size, the adjoining gardens and fields, the family house will be well suited for this.[15] There will be no difficulty in giving this over to the Sisters of St. Charles.

We were brought up in the old-fashioned school. Our parents were both deeply Christian. While our father from morning to night supervised the apprentices and workers, of which there were at times five or six in the house, our mother never missed a day hearing Mass. She always took with her one or the other of the children who was not yet in school. She went to Holy Communion often and fasted not only on the fast days of the Church but at other times as well; my father, however, did not approve of this. In my case there was needed at times the promise of a penny or something similar to bring me to Mass, Rosary and Stations of the Cross. This was the occasion for one of my companions to say to his mother, who called his attention to my zeal in going to church: "Give me a penny every day and I will be like him."

On All Saints [Nov. 1], 1818,[16] I began going to our village school. Since the Lord gave me a good memory I was always one of the first for the six years.[17] However, the fact that my father always held one or the other of the town offices may have had some influence on the teacher.[18] During these years I had acquired from my father, who was a great lover of books, a decided passion for reading. As a result the time that others spent in sports or bird catching I spent in reading all the books I could get hold of.[19] This is the reason why my mother often called me the little Bookworm.

When I was seven I began to go to confession, and I was

confirmed in the summer of 1819 by the Bishop of Budweis.[20] People could not remember when a bishop had come to our remote mountain village. This is why the crowd of people and the celebration were beyond description and remained so vivid in my memory that since then I have had not the least trouble recalling the smallest details. About the day of my First Holy Communion I can recall nothing, for in Bohemia it is not the custom to celebrate First Holy Communions as solemnly as in other countries. If I recall rightly, I was not yet ten when I was thoroughly familiar with the Large Catechism[21] and was also admitted then to First Holy Communion along with the other older First Communicants. After that, we all went every three months.

I cannot say that I felt a decided inclination for the priesthood when I was a child. I had, of course, a little altar made of lead, and served Mass almost every day. However, my idea of the priesthood was so exalted that it seemed beyond my reach.[22] We had an old servant in the house, one who was strict in her observance of fasting. One day when, in keeping with the family practice, I said the prayers before meals out loud, and through forgetfulness made a Latin cross instead of the three crosses, one each on the forehead, mouth and breast,[23] she said: "See, our little John is going to be a priest." My mother spoke of this incident on various occasions because she hoped that I would one day be a priest. However, the thought came to me repeatedly later on, especially when our other school companions made up their minds regarding [further] studies and, as was the custom with us, first took lessons in Latin for a year or two from our Catechist. I too was asked about this and my parents agreed to this at once. And so, the last two years of school, 1822-1823, I went every night with eight or ten others to the Catechist to learn the rudiments of Latin.[24]

On All Saints, 1823, I went with about twenty others from our town to Budweis for study at the *Gymnasium* under the

Piarist Fathers.[25] Since I was anxious not to cause my parents unnecessary expenses, I took a room with board with three others.[26] Both were very cheap and cost no more than $16.00 for the ten months.[27] I had very little to learn because the Catechist at home had taught us so much in the few hours each week that, with little preparation, we could have been admitted at once into the third year. However, that was not permitted us. I was accustomed to fill up the many idle hours and days with nothing else but the reading of all sorts of books that I could get my hands on, without thinking of being selective. At times I gladly went out to play or went for a walk with students from back home, but this happened only seldom. The two elderly people with whom I lived were very good Christians, but they had no control over us. Moreover, since we got a professor who, because of his advanced age and easy going ways, was also given to drink, we did not make progress in our studies. Actually, I even forgot a great deal of what I had formerly known. In our third year this unfortunate priest appeared drunk at the examinations in the presence of the Head Master and was dismissed.[28] Shortly after that he shot himself to death.

His successor was just as learned, and [he was] strict. In half a year he wanted to cover again the subjects of [the past] two and a half years.[29] Considering the lazy ways we had taken on under his predecessor, this was too much for most of the students. As a result, many dropped out. I was even more dissatisfied with the Religion professor who was dryness and dullness personified. He had an obsession for every word and I did not have a good word-for-word memory. As a result, to me the two classes in religion were most boring.

We went to confession every three months. As far as I can recall, it was always a truly serious matter with me to receive the holy sacraments properly, for the first instruction that I received in my home town and the recollection of the piety in my family home kept me from the pitfalls in which most of my school companions were trapped. At the end of the [school] year, 1827, I was very disgusted with my studies and during the vacation I even thought about giving them up. In this situation I readily let my mother and my deceased sister [Veronica] talk me into continuing them.[30] Actually, the study of the Humanities was much more to my liking, because we had a professor who, although stricter than the other, nevertheless manifested a certain amount of condescension towards us.[31]

During the two years of philosophy (Nov. 1, 1829 -Sept. 7, 1831) many changes took place in me. We were a group of eight or ten students who showed a strong attraction for various areas of study.[32] We spent all our free hours and entire recreation days sharing with one another what each one had found out in his own specialty.[33] Added to this, there was the good and blameless conduct of our professors, the revered Cistercians, who were in charge of the Institute of Philosophy.[34] With them everyone felt a very friendly welcome and complete satisfaction despite the fact that they were mercilessly strict when they discovered deceit or bad will.

In those two years I avidly followed my bent for the natural sciences: botany and biology, geography, physics, geology, astronomy.[35] And I applied myself with the greatest enthusiasm to algebra, geometry, and trigonometry, subjects that formerly were not to my liking.[36] When the time came, at the end of the philosophy course, for me to decide either for theology, or law or medicine, I felt more of an attraction for the latter. This was all the more so because out of eighty or ninety applicants for theology, only twenty were to be accepted. For this, along with the best scholastic transcript, recommendations were also required, and I wanted to have nothing to do with them.[37]

In this uncertainty about the choice of a profession, I came home in the autumn vacation of 1831 and found that my father was not against letting me study medicine in Prague, even though the expenses involved were great. My mother was not too happy with this. Even though I pointed out to her that I did not know anyone who would back my request for admission into the institute for the study of theology (everyone studied there without paying tuition), nevertheless she thought that I should give it a try. I then wrote a letter of application and sent it to Budweis by a special messenger to the bishop's consistory and shortly after that I received the letter of acceptance into the Budweis Theological Seminary. From that moment on I never gave another thought to medicine and I also practically gave up completely the study of physics and astronomy on which I preferred to spend time, and this without any great difficulty.[38] The studies pursued up to the present had at least this good result, that I had not wasted my time on trivialities and that my mind was better prepared for the serious study of theology.[39] During the philosophy [years] I also went to church even on weekdays; actually, most of my companions at that time did likewise.

On the feast of All Saints, 1831, I began the study of theology. At that time, because of the lack of space in the diocesan seminary, only those in the last two years were allowed to live in. Consequently, I was an extern.[40] I studied *con amore* Sacred Scripture (Old Testament), Hebrew and Church History.[41] I did this to my own personal satisfaction and also to the satisfaction of my professors who were diocesan priests and who, with the exception of the professor of Church History and Canon Law who was more of a Josephinist,[42] had a good spirit and with great ease taught us in a short time a great deal of useful material. At the end of the first year of theology I was one of the few who were to receive Tonsure and the four Minor Orders.[43] This actually took place on July 21, 1832.

In the second year of theology we had the New Testament in Latin and Greek together with Exegesis and Canon Law. What appealed to me most were the Letters of the Apostle, St.

Paul, which the professor knew how to explain very well.[44] About this time I began to read the reports of the Leopoldine Society,[45] especially the letters of Father Baraga[46] and other missionaries among the Germans in North America. This is how there arose in one of my fellow students, Adalbert Schmidt, and in myself on the occasion of a walk along the Moldau River, the determination to devote ourselves to North America as soon as we acquired some experience after ordination. Two or three of our fellow students, whom we invited to join us, marvelled at our decision, but they did not want to promise anything.[47] Obviously, it was not their vocation. From that moment on my resolution was so strong and lively that I could no longer think of anything else.

We had talks on how to carry out our project. We thought it would be better for me to try to obtain from the bishop of Budweis the recently vacated foundation scholarship at the University of Prague[48] for a theologian from the Budweis seminary. [We did this] in the hope of easily learning French and English there because we thought that the knowledge of these languages was much more important than is actually the case.[49] The bishop granted my request, but I found myself very much disappointed. I had hardly gone to the French classes at the *Clementinum*[50] for a few [days or weeks] when an order came from the archbishop that no seminarian was to attend these classes.[51] As for English, I could learn even less because that language was not taught at the University then.[52]

At Prague I was likewise displeased with the professors of Dogmatic and Moral Theology as well as of Pastoral Theology.[53] The first was more against the Pope than for him, but he raised so many ridiculous difficulties that he was too little regarded to do any harm. The second was far too philosophical for a single one of us to understand him. The third was an out and out Josephinist.[54] It cost me a great deal of effort and self conquest to study subjects and opinions, the foolishness of which I had already learned to see through.[55] It is a pity that, in institutions like this, so much [more] is done to keep up the appearance of learning than to spread good Catholic and useful knowledge. I was, obviously, genuinely happy when I could return to Budweis in August, 1835,[56] after having passed the examination successfully.[57]

Meanwhile, the bishop of Philadelphia, Fr.[ancis] P.[atrick] Kenrick (the present archbishop of Baltimore)[58] empowered Dr. Räss, the rector of the Strassburg seminary (now bishop of Strassburg), to accept young priests or, even better, theologians for his diocese. The latter wrote to a very saintly priest, who was Vicar of the Budweis Cathedral, about the possibility of getting some of them from Bohemia. Through a special disposition of divine providence this turned out to be the one (Father Hermann Dichtl) who brought the Order of the Sisters of St. Charles of Nancy to Bohemia. He also happened to be the confessor of my friend Adalbert Schmidt and knew about our proposal to go to America.[59] Aside from three or four of our fellow students and him, no one knew about this. He was very happy to discover in us the first two that he found ready to go to America. Furthermore, on his trip to France to bring three postulants to Nancy to the above-mentioned Sisters, he became acquainted with the genuinely *Catholic Paris Foreign Mission Society.*[60] And since he was a man who had in abundance the mind and the courage to take in big plans and carry them through, he thought about setting up a similar Institute in Austria. The request to Dr. Räss, mentioned above, and our own decision seemed to be signs that his plan would be feasible. Since the bishop, who was over eighty, was sick, and since, for four or five months, there was no prospect that he would hold an ordination,[61] he was all in favor of the two of us being ready to take off as soon as possible.[62] His plan, however, met with no approval at all, not only from the bishop but from the Cathedral Chapter as well.[63]

The Leopoldine Society, from which we requested the necessary traveling expenses, refused because they said that the bishop of Philadelphia should have requested it for us and not we ourselves. Despite such bad prospects, the Vicar of the Cathedral arranged for the bishop to communicate our proposal to many of the pastors and allow them to take up a collection among the priests of the diocese. However, because there was no mention of a recommendation or even of only a wish on his part, the amount gathered was scarcely sufficient to cover traveling expenses for one. It was then decided that I should set out by myself.[64] Moreover, since Dr. Räss had promised each missionary going to America four to five hundred francs as a supplement to the traveling expenses, all difficulties seemed settled. After many requests and letters, the passport finally came, good for three years.[65] My father gave his consent reluctantly; my mother by contrast seemed pleased.[66] I likewise found all encouragement possible from the clergy of our town and especially the Dean.—After I made a pilgrimage to Nepomuc, the birthplace of my Patron Saint,[67] I left my home town on February 8, 1836, without taking a formal farewell.[68]

The necessary preparations for travel kept me in Budweis several more days. On the 13th, after receiving the bishop's blessing,[69] I set out for Linz. My friend, Adalbert Schmidt, accompanied me to the outskirts of his home town which was on my way.[70] On our route through the Bohemian forest the snow was fourteen or fifteen feet high. In Linz I stayed at the diocesan seminary and was honored by Bishop Ziegler with a Latin address and a sumptuous meal. At that time a missionary, even one *in spe*, was regarded as something unusual; that was not an everyday event. Provided with letters of recommendation,[71] I left Linz in the evening of February 18th for Munich. On the way we passed through Altötting. However, since it was dark I could hardly make out the celebrated pilgrimage church.[72] In

Munich I stayed with my cousin, Philip Janson, who is a member of the Royal *Hartschier* Bodyguard.[73]

When I went to Dr. Phillips, the Professor,[74] I met Father Henni (the Vicar General of Cincinnati and present bishop of Milwaukee). He gave me the strange news that the bishop of Philadelphia had just revoked the authorization he gave Dr. Räss to accept missionaries for his diocese and that, as a result, I had no hope of being accepted by him.[75] Professor Phillips volunteered to write to Bishop Bruté of Vincennes, who had recently passed through Munich on his way to Rome, and ask if he would be willing to receive me into his diocese.[76] I was to remain in Strassburg until the answer arrived. In Augsburg, where I arrived on the 21st of February, I received a most hospitable welcome from Dean Fischert of the Cathedral Chapter and his Chaplain, Dr. Schmidt.[77] The latter joined the Jesuits at Freiburg later on.

When I came to Strassburg at the end of February,[78] Dr. Räss also told me that I could not go to Philadelphia,[79] that he would write to Bishop Dubois of New York about accepting me[80] because Bishop Bruté probably would not be able to accept me. A more urgent bit of news was the fact that he had already given away to other missionaries from Alsace and Lorraine the traveling money that had been marked for me. Meanwhile he promised to write a rich merchant in Paris on my behalf who, as a great friend of the missions, would undoubtedly see that I received a goodly subsidy. Since my traveling money was a source of concern for him, he advised me to go to Paris immediately and to wait there for the answer from Bishop Bruté.[81]

Hence I left Strassburg on March 3rd and visited the hospital of the Sisters of St. Charles in Nancy[82] where I also met two of the novices that Father Dichtl had brought there. I had known both of them in Budweis and they were very happy to hear some news from far away Bohemia. Here I also met a priest from Alsace who likewise wanted to go to America and who had written about this to Bishop Bruté and planned to wait for the answer in Paris.[83] I was very happy about this because he was a very holy and zealous priest and spoke French fluently while I, despite my good school report in French, had trouble now and then in understanding a word or in making myself understood.[84] The two of us arrived in Paris on the Saturday before *Laetare* Sunday.[85]

Despite all the testimonials and recommendations from Strassburg, we were unable to find lodgings with the Sulpicians,[86] and, after many refusals, we were finally received in the Foreign Missions Seminary[87] on the condition that we pay the twenty francs for the monthly rent of the room. We had to take our meals in the guest house. The reason for all this discrimination towards us was the bad reputation that had befallen all German priests of that time because of the petition of the clergy of Baden and Wurttenburg for the abolition of celibacy.[88] The rich merchant of Strassburg was not to be found, and my traveling money had dwindled to about two hundred francs.[89]

Although no answer had as yet arrived from Bishop Bruté,[90] I started out on my journey[91] with my two leather bags and big box full of books (a present from Dr. Räss). When I came to Messagerie Lafitte & Co. to leave for Havre, my stagecoach had already left about five minutes earlier. To catch up with it, and so as not to lose the twenty-four francs [already paid], I was advised to hire a hack to catch up with the stagecoach.[92] However, I was too late, and the driver, to whom I had paid five francs, left me [standing] outside Paris on the road to Havre de Grace. I did not want to go back and so, trusting my two good feet, in good spirits I marched along the way leading to the ocean even though the sun had already set. It became darker by the minute and, to make matters worse, it began to rain steadily. As a result I arrived at St. Germain by way of Nanterre completely drenched from my night march but not the least bit tired.

Here I met a good old Frenchman who must have noticed my difficulty. When, after a hundred "Whats," and two hundred "If you please," I got him to understand my predicament, he went to the office of Messagerie Lafitte and shortly after that he helped me up the covered roof of the high stagecoach on which I came to Havre by way of Rouen behind the driver's seat and sitting next to a Jew.[93] I only had to pay the conductor a small amount.

After my arrival in Havre[94] (on the 9th of March),[95] on my first trip to the harbor I found at once the American three-master, "The Europe," and Captain Drummond. With the help of an interpreter I came to an agreement with him to take me to New York on the middle deck for eighty francs.[96] Since I obviously had to provide my own food, for fifty-six more francs I bought potatoes, biscuits, salt, oil, butter and ham, and finally a cooking pot, etc., and a straw mattress. On the 10th, my luggage that had been left behind in Paris arrived and at the same time the news came from Father Schaefer (my travel companion from Nancy to Paris) that he, but not I, was accepted by the bishop of Vincennes.[97] On the same day I had my things brought on board and I also lived there until we weighed anchor about two o'clock in the afternoon of April 20th and sailed out into the channel.[98]

The ocean voyage lasted until Trinity Sunday when we anchored at the New York quarantine.[99] Nothing outstanding took place except that once, in a raging wind that hit the topmast, I was almost struck dead; it crashed on the very spot of the deck that I had left scarcely a minute earlier. Although the company aboard was not choice (mostly Protestants from the canton of Berne) and although we had a lot of contrary wind, this ocean voyage meant a great deal to me; moreover, only a few times did I have an attack of seasickness.[100] Because we had no sick on board, we had no difficulty passing over to Long Island on Monday in a sloop and going to New York from there on the steamship "Columbus."[101]

Bishop Dubois of New York[102] was very happy over my arrival,[103] for he was in great need of German priests. I lived in his house and, while I was waiting for ordination,[104] Father Raffeiner assigned me the task of preparing the children of the German parish for First Holy Communion.[105] On the 19th of June in St. Patrick's Cathedral, Bishop Dubois ordained me sub-deacon; on the 24th, the feast of St. John the Baptist, deacon; and on the 25th, priest.[106] On the 26th, a Sunday, I celebrated the High Mass in St. Nicholas' Church on Second Street (N.Y.) as my first Holy Mass and during it I gave First Holy Communion to the children whom I had prepared.[107]

Even before my arrival, the bishop had selected me for Williamsville in Erie County, N.Y., and requested that I set out at once. On the journey[108] I said Mass on the feast of Sts. Peter and Paul, which was still a holy day of obligation at that time, in St. Mary's, Albany, and in the morning of the 4th of July I arrived at Rochester where, in keeping with the wishes of the bishop, I was to spend a few days. The (old) St. Joseph's Church[109] was not yet ready for divine service and so I had to make use of my priestly faculties for the first time in St. Patrick's.[110] I preached there twice on Sunday, heard confessions and baptized, all this for the first time in America.[111] On the 10th of July Father Prost came to Rochester. The bishop had invited him to take over the German communities, but had not expected him so soon.[112] I remained another day with that zealous priest because he wanted me to. He was the first Redemptorist with whom I had the opportunity to speak.[113]

On the 13th I said Mass in Buffalo[114] in the old (frame) St. Louis' Church where Father Pax had been for a year.[115] Later the same day he brought me out to Williamsville (ten miles north of Buffalo).[116] From here, along with the Williamsville parish, I also took care of the parish in North Bush and a third in Lancaster (Cayuga) for a whole year. I also began to visit the community in Transit and Batavia as well as a German settlement in Niagara County along the Erie Canal below Pendleton.[117]

Since I had to fire the school teacher of Williamsville for bad conduct, and since the communities were not in a position to hire a new teacher because of the churches and school that were being built, and even more because of their poverty, I conducted school in Williamsville for six or seven months until a teacher was again installed.[118] In my first fervor I worked a bit too hard at that time and drew down upon myself repeated admonitions from Father Pax.[119] Since I was obliged, or rather expected, to pay my board in Williamsville, and had a debt of eighty dollars after a year,[120] I changed my regular residence to North Bush where I lived with a farmer in his log cabin for a year and a half.[121] I lived there for nothing and was very highly regarded, but I also had to walk every day almost a mile and a half through the muddy woods to the nearest church.[122]

In the summer of 1837 Bishop Dubois came to my parishes on his episcopal visitation; he was accompanied by Father Prost.[123] The latter would have liked very much to get the bishop to give over Buffalo and my parishes to the Congregation of the Most Holy Redeemer.[124] To facilitate this project he exhorted me often and at length to enter his Congregation. His reasons were all very good and true, but they did not impress me because at that time I did not have a spark of a vocation. The bishop did not want to know or hear a thing about Father Prost's proposal[125] and so the latter gave up even the Rochester parish and went to Norwalk, Ohio.[126] A few weeks previously Father Hätscher also visited me in North Bush, and even though I had a great liking for him as well as for Father Chakert [Czackert],[127] whom I once met in Buffalo on a passing visit, I never got the thought of entering the Congregation.

I then received the invitation to go to Rochester and take care of that parish also until a priest was found.[128] I was astounded at the tremendous amount of good that Father Prost had accomplished in such a short time. The fervor shown in making visits to the church, the frequent practice of confessions by men and young people—all of which he accomplished through the introduction of the Fraternity of Mt. Carmel—made the most profound impression on me.[129] Convinced of the good results of the Fraternity, I wanted to introduce it into my parishes also and I asked Father Prost for his advice.[130] His answer was that he had the power to introduce it as a member of the Congregation of the Most Holy Redeemer, but that he could not impart the power to others.[131] He ended his letter with a repeated explanation of the phrase, *Vae Soli.* ["Woe to him who is alone."][132]

On the order of Bishop Dubois, a certain Father Lutgen (from Luxemburg) took over Lancaster and Williamsville. However, this did not last long. A few days after his arrival, there came some derogatory letters about him. His preaching against ecclesiastical superiors and confession, etc., and even more, his association with women, resulted in his being suspended by the bishop after four or five weeks.[133] Once again I had to take over these fast growing parishes. Meanwhile my people in North Bush built me a little frame house next to the church, set up a little garden and in this way made my living conditions much easier.[134] Furthermore, this took place when, at the end of September, 1838, my brother Wenceslaus came here and took upon himself the house duties, for which I had never hired anyone up until then.[135] However, my duties increased daily because I now had to care for Sheldon also.[136] After I made visits to Rochester every two or three months, Father Sänderl settled there.[137] About Easter, 1840, I was taken by a very persistent and recurring fever and suffered from it for three months.[138] After I was somewhat restored, it was recommended that I take a short trip and so I went to Rochester to visit Father Sänderl whom I did not yet know. After staying with him three or four days I returned to my mission.[139] During that time, neither Father Sänderl nor I spoke about entering the Congregation, or even thought about it.

For four years now I had spared myself no pain to bring the parishes under my care to a fervor similar to that which I observed at St. Joseph's parish in Rochester. But, things would not go that way. This, as well as a natural, or rather supernatural, desire to live in a community of priests, where I would not have to be exposed alone to the thousand dangers of the world, made me suddenly resolve to request from Father Prost, who remained in Baltimore after the Provincial Council of 1840,[140] admittance into the Congregation of the Most Holy Redeemer. I wrote to him that very day, in fact that very hour (Sept. 4, 1840) and I received from him [the news of my] acceptance in a letter of the 16th of September from Baltimore.[141] Immediately after receiving the letter, I made my decision known· to the Administrator of the Diocese, Bishop Hughes. I also asked him, along with his blessing, to provide the parish with one of our priests. After I waited fourteen days, in vain, for an answer (he was away on Visitation but I did not know that), I made my travel preparations and left my stations, I believe, on the 8th or 9th of October.[142] I left my brother Wenceslaus behind to gather up the few small possessions of mine scattered over the different missions and then to follow me to Pittsburgh.

In Buffalo I waited until the 13th when, at eight o'clock in the evening, I was able to procure standing room, not sitting room or, much less, sleeping room on a small steamer that already had over four hundred emigrants and passengers on board. A terrible storm came up about midnight and the weak, overloaded boat could not master it. When, after a long, wretched night, we looked about us in the morning, we found that we were back again outside the Buffalo harbor. Without landing, the captain took on another load of coal and as soon as the wind let up a bit he sailed out again on the lake. This was still very rough and, instead of being in Erie at noon, by two o'clock we had only reached Dunkirk.[143] Here the captain, without landing, again took on board a load of pit-coal from boats that were passing by. In the night between October 14th and 15th, the storm broke out again when we were almost at Erie. Since the captain feared the shoals close-by, he changed course and about three or four o'clock in the morning we were again back at Dunkirk where we had been twelve hours earlier. However, at daybreak the bad weather was over and about two o'clock in the afternoon on the feast of St. Theresa [Oct. 15th], we all landed in Erie. Since we left Buffalo we had eaten nothing, for we never thought about taking provisions along because we presumed that we would have put the ninety miles behind us before daybreak. The incessant rain, the seasickness, etc., etc., the complete lack of rest and sleep left us all completely drained.

In Erie I met Father Ivo Leviz, a Franciscan, who took care of the small German parish. I rested at his place for a day and then in the evening of the 16th I departed for Pittsburgh on the stagecoach. I arrived there on the morning of the 18th and [received] a friendly welcome from Father Tschenhens, the Superior of the house.[144] Since it was a Sunday I was invited to celebrate the High Mass in the Factory Church.[145] Father Czackert took care of the small missions out in the country.[146] As Father Tschenhens was called to Baltimore on All Saints, under the Superiorship of Father Czackert, who was often absent, I had to take care of the [home] parish. On the evening of November 29th Father Prost (at that time he was still the General Superior in America) arrived to invest me with the habit. However, he left his book behind in Baltimore and made up [an investiture ceremony] from his memory and from his head, and I was solemnly invested according to that ceremony on the feast of St. Andrew after the High Mass.[147] At that time there was no novice master or novitiate in America and too much work.[148] Consequently, every day I made, along with the

others, the two community meditations, examinations [of con-
science], spiritual reading, visits [to the Blessed Sacrament],
the Rosary. And that was all.[149]

In the week before Easter the new Superior [in America],
Father Alexander [Czvitkovicz][150] came to Pittsburgh with Father Alig and Frater Fey.[151] Father Prost went to Baltimore for a
time and returned to Pittsburgh where he was [local] Superior
for a while after Father Alexander left.[152] In the middle of May,
1841, I was supposed to go to Baltimore to begin my novitiate
there. However, when I first arrived there on the 21st with Frater
Fey and Brother Wenceslaus, Fathers Alexander, Rumpler,
Cartuyvels, along with several Brothers, lived there in such
cramped quarters that in a few days I received the order to go to
New York and help Father [Nicholaus] Balleis [O.S.B.] (in St.
Nicholas on Second Street). This lasted fourteen days.

Then the order came for me to go to Rochester to make at
least some kind of a novitiate under the guidance of Father
Tschenhens. However, I was hardly there when a letter came
to him [telling him] to return to Norwalk in Ohio[153] where a
certain Father Farigny [?] had started a schism. As a result I
was alone for two months with Brother Louis[154] until Fathers
Sänderl and Prost came from Pittsburgh and Buffalo towards
the end of July. Because Father Pax in Buffalo was sick, I was
sent there to help him.[155] He too would have liked to give the
Buffalo parish over to the Congregation. However, Bishop
Hughes was not in favor of this[156] and Father Alexander appeared unwilling to compromise himself since he did not have
the corresponding faculties for this from Vienna.

When Father Pax was restored to health I was recalled
to Rochester on September 9th, 1841, and stayed there only
a few days. The reason was that Father Tschenhens had too
much work in Ohio and I was due to help him. So, on September
16th I went to Norwalk and took care of St. Alphonsus' parish[157]
while Father Tschenhens was practically always traveling,

making the rounds of the missions of the scattered Germans in northern Ohio. About the middle of November, 1841, Father Alexander ordered me to set out for Baltimore to make my novitiate there.[158] On the way he allowed me to give missions here and there.

Under continual downpours, traveling in an open stage-coach, I arrived at [?][159] on November 17th and at Canton on the 19th. Here I met Bishop Purcell of Cincinnati[160] with his Vicar General, Father Henni, on visitation. Since the rumor was then widespread that our Congregation in America was near dissolution,[161] they both extended to me a very pressing invitation to go to Cincinnati. When I declined, I was asked to visit the German parish in Randolph where one of the factions had burned down the church three years before and where, because of this, there was no priest there since. I stayed there about ten days and although the weather was very cold, practically all came to church every day and all, almost without exception, received the holy sacraments.[162]

On the trip to Wheeling I became sick on the stagecoach and stayed two days in a house on the way about ten miles from Steubenville (Oh.). The people there—Americans without any particular religion—nursed me with the greatest care and without taking a penny. In Steubenville (Oh.) I stayed over Sunday with the few Germans whom I had already visited many times from Pittsburgh.[163] I then traveled to Baltimore by way of Wheeling and Cumberland, arriving there on the feast of Mary's Immaculate Conception [Dec. 8th]. At that time the entire journey had to be made by stagecoach as far as Frederick [Md.]; it was only from there that one could go by railroad.[164]

Here in Baltimore the Fathers had already moved to St. James' because they were in the process of tearing down St. John's and the small adjoining house.[165] I made the novitiate then with Father Bayer;[166] every day we made the daily exercises as far as we knew them. For the care of souls, which was not heavy then, Fathers Alexander, Rumpler and Fey[167] were more than enough. This [set-up] did not last long. After making the Spiritual Exercises for fourteen days, I made my vows in the hands of Father Alexander on the 16th of January, 1842, in St. James' Church, Baltimore.[168] Thus my novitiate was ended.

Father Rumpler went to New York, Father Bayer to Rochester, and Father Alexander to Europe. Consequently, Father Fey, the Superior, and I cared for the whole parish.[169] The number of school children, boys and girls, was never greater than ninety. I was present when Canon Salzbacher of Vienna, with the permission of Archbishop Eccleston, laid the foundation stone of the present St. Alphonsus' Church on May 1, 1842.[170] As a rule the care of the stations out in the country came to me. We took care of Cumberland, Harpers Ferry, Martinsburg, Richmond, Frederick, York, Columbia, Strassburg [Strassburg = Shrewsbury] regularly and of many other places occasionally.[171]

On the 5th of March, 1844, Father Alexander made me Superior of our house in Pittsburgh where Father Cartuyvels had laid the foundation stone for St. Philomena's Church the previous Corpus Christi and had begun the building.[172] Father Fey had come to Pittsburgh to take his place but he only stayed until the 1st of March.[173] In Pittsburgh I lived with Fathers Tschenhens, Müller, Kronenburg, and Schaefler, Hatz and Seelos.[174] Only two or three of these were home regularly [at a time]. For the most part I was occupied with the building of the church[175] until January 25th, 1847, when Father Czackert called me to Baltimore because of a prolonged illness.[176] On the occasion of the visitation by Father [De] Held, he had been made the Superior General in America.[177] From then on I remained mostly in Baltimore.

On the 9th of February, 1847, the letter arrived in which Father [De] Held (Provincial of the Congregation of the Most Holy Redeemer in Belgium) named me his Vicar. I held this office until the arrival of the present Provincial, Father Bernard Hafkenscheid.[178]

On April 1, 1851, I was installed as the First Rector of St. Alphonsus' community in Baltimore.[179]

On February 1, 1852, His Holiness, Pope Pius IX, named me bishop of Philadelphia. On the evening of the feast of St. Joseph, the Archbishop of Baltimore, Dr. Kenrick, received the Papal Bull, and he brought it to the house the next day.[180]

Tomorrow, on March 28th, my birthday, that is Passion Sunday this year (1852), if nothing happens in the meantime, I will be consecrated in St. Alphonsus' Church.[181]

But You, O God, Have Mercy on Us.
Thanks be to God and Mary.

Baltimore, March 27, 1852.
Passion of Christ Strengthen me.[182]
John Nep. Neumann, C.SS.R.
Bishop-Elect of Philadelphia

Epilogue:

The Philadelphia Years and the Cause of Canonization

The autobiography of John Neumann covers his life up to the time when he became bishop of Philadelphia. At the end of the autobiography we read: "On February 1, 1852, His Holiness, Pius IX, named me bishop of Philadelphia.... Tomorrow, on March 28th, my birthday, that is Passion Sunday this year (1852), if nothing happens in the meantime, I will be consecrated in St. Alphonsus' Church."

His Episcopal Ordination

Archbishop Francis Patrick Kenrick of Baltimore played the leading role in the promotion of Neumann as bishop of Philadelphia. Before going to Baltimore in 1851 he was bishop of Philadelphia. He had known Neumann previously. In Baltimore he used to take the short walk to St. Alphonsus' to go to confession to Neumann and to seek spiritual direction from a truly holy priest. He came to know Neumann and see at first-hand his zeal, learning and holiness. As archbishop, Kenrick had to take the lead in arranging for a bishop in one of his suffragan Sees. He found that man in John Neumann.

The views of other archbishops and bishops were sought. All agreed that Neumann was endowed with the necessary learning and holiness; not all agreed that Neumann, a foreign born, was the man for the outstanding See of Philadelphia. In the official list of three candidates that he sent to Rome, Kenrick put Neumann's name second. This was in deference to views expressed by some of his fellow bishops. In letters to Rome in which he expressed privately his personal opinion, he said that Neumann was the most worthy of the three and that his name should be first. When the appointment of Neumann came through, Kenrick could tell his brother, Archbishop Peter Richard Kenrick of St. Louis: "I wish without delay to make you a partner of my joy. The Pope named John Neumann, a very holy man, to be my successor in the See of Philadelphia."

When Neumann heard about the rumor that his name had been proposed, he was terrified. He wrote to his Superiors in Europe to do all that they could to prevent the appointment. Despite the reports of his confreres, the Cardinals decided to petition the Pope to name John Neumann for the See. On February 1, Pius IX appointed Neumann the new bishop of Philadelphia. He dispensed him from his Redemptorist vow of poverty that obliged him to refuse such a dignity; he made him bishop under obedience without any possibility of appeal. How Neumann first found out he was bishop makes an interesting story. When Kenrick got the news from Rome, he walked to St. Alphonsus'. Finding Neumann out, he left his own archiepiscopal cross and ring on Neumann's desk. Neumann got the message. In a letter to his family he says: "I knew indeed what that meant and when I visited him the next day, he [Kenrick] let me read the letter." Because the First Plenary Council of Baltimore was to be held in May, Rome was anxious that Neumann be ordained bishop as soon as possible. The archbishop set the date for Passion Sunday, March 28, and left the other arrangements in the hands of

Father Bernard Hafkenscheid, the Redemptorist Provincial.

Besides Archbishop Kenrick, Bishop Bernard O'Reilly of Hartford took part in the ordination of his earlier co-worker and friend. On his way to Buffalo, after being ordained by Bishop Dubois as a diocesan priest of New York in 1836, Neumann stopped off at Rochester where Father O'Reilly was pastor of St. Patrick's, the only church. There in "the Irish church" Neumann "made use of his priestly faculties for the first time" as he ministered to Father O'Reilly's German parishioners. The bond of friendship remained warm through the years. With the diocesan seminarians and the Redemptorist novices and seminarians doing the singing, the parishioners at St. Alphonsus' witnessed the beautiful liturgical ceremony of the episcopal ordination of their pastor. It took place on his forty-first birthday, and he chose as his episcopal motto the words: "Passion of Christ, strengthen me."

The Diocese of Philadelphia

Accompanied by Father Hafkenscheid, other Redemptorists, along with priests from Philadelphia, Neumann made a very quiet entrance into his diocese on Tuesday, March 30, 1852. Probably at the suggestion of Father Edward Sourin, the plans for a large reception with a parade were called off. With the money saved in this way, plans were made to build a new school. This delighted Neumann, the retiring man with a driving zeal for schools. A group of priests greeted him at the station. Neumann said to them: "Oh, how I thank you for this quiet but cordial welcome. It was just what I wanted." Later he met the people when they crowded St. John's, the pro-cathedral. Neumann had entered his diocese.

The vast diocese of 35,000 square miles took in all Eastern Pennsylvania, the state of Delaware and the section of New Jersey from Trenton to Cape May. The diocese of Neumann in

1852 is now the present archdiocese of Philadelphia along with
dioceses of Trenton, Camden, Wilmington, Harrisburg, Allen-
town and part of Altoona-Johnstown. Over a million people
lived there, of whom 170,000 were Catholics. The city of
Philadelphia had a population of 400,000; Philadelphia and its
environs numbered 90,000 Catholics. The diocese had ninety-
two churches, eight chapels, one-hundred-one priests, forty-
three seminarians, two colleges, six academies for girls and
seven charitable institutions. Besides the group of diocesan
priests, he had the Augustinians, Jesuits, Vincentians and
Redemptorists. The diocese had its own seminary. The Madams
of the Sacred Heart, the Visitation Sisters and the Sisters of St.
Joseph conducted academies for girls. There were three colleges: St. Joseph's conducted by the Jesuits, Villanova by the
Augustinians, and St. Mary's in Wilmington founded by Father
Patrick Reilly. The diocese was provided with a hospital conducted by the Sisters of St. Joseph, a House of the Good
Shepherd, three homes for orphans and a home for widows
conducted by the Sisters of Charity and the Sisters of St. Joseph.
Neumann's task was to build up on Kenrick's foundation.

Neumann had to build up in changing circumstances.
While the city of Philadelphia continued to grow and grow,
places like Wilmington, Chester, Reading, York, Columbia,
Easton and Scranton were seeing the growth of "Catholic clus-
ters." One still must reckon with the remote and outlying
settlements where Catholics lived miles apart. The big change
during these years was the tremendous influx of immigrants
from Europe: Irish, Germans and then Italians. Some got no
further than Philadelphia where they began to border on the
neighborhoods of the wealthy and long-established Catholic
families. Others found their way throughout the diocese. The
Irish tended to settle in the mining districts of Scranton,
Wilkes-Barre and Pottsville in the northeast; the Germans
gravitated to the farming districts of York, Lancaster and

Original first page of the "autobiography" (copy)

(Redemptorist Provincial Archives, Baltimore Province)

(above): "The Neumann Room"—St. Alphonsus Rectory, Baltimore, Maryland. Here Neumann wrote the "autobiography" on the evening of March 27, 1852, and in the same room, three weeks earlier, he discovered the pectoral cross and ring of Archbishop Kenrick, silent notice of his elevation to the see of Philadelphia. The room is still intact in the present church rectory. This photograph was taken *circa* 1900.

(below): John Neumann as a young boy.

Our Mother daily heard mass to which she took one of us.

John Neumann: The Neumann Photograph.

The art of photography was in its infancy during John Neumann's lifetime (1811-1860), but two portrait photo-graphs were made of him—one in 1852 and the other in 1855.

Neumann sat for the 1852 portrait under obedience to his Redemptorist Superiors who had the foresight of anticipating the value of such a picture; the photograph was taken in Baltimore, in March of that year, at the time of his Episcopal Consecration. Concerning the 1855 portrait: Neumann went to Rome in 1854 for the promulgation of the Dogma of Mary's Immaculate Conception (December 8, 1854); while in Europe, Neumann visited his hometown (Prachatitz, Bohemia), and was prevailed upon by his friends to sit for the second photo-graph, which was taken in Munich, in February, 1855—the friends used the ploy of promising to sell copies of the portrait and to give the proceeds to the poor.

The photograph accompanying these notes was recently discovered in a book of memorabilia in the Archives of the Redemptorists in Brooklyn, N.Y. However, there is no certainty as to whether it is the first or second portrait. In this reproduction of the original, nothing about Neumann's body or clothing has been retouched. However, because of the difficulty of distinguishing his facial outline from the background of the original, Neumann's form has been cut-out and laid against a lightened background.

In this photograph, Neumann is seen wearing the traditional Redemptorist black habit and the other extras that go with it: white linen collar, wrap-around cincture-belt, fifteen decade rosary to which is attached a bronze medallion. The last item is distinguished by having on one side an image of Jesus the Redeemer bearing a large cross; this is surmounted by the legend "Copiosa Apud Eum Redemptio" ("In him, there is plentiful redemption"—Psalm 130). On the other side of the medallion there is an image of St. Alphonsus Liguori, founder of the Redemptorists. Around Neumann's neck is a long chain to which is attached the Episcopal Cross, which he has

inserted into his cincture (usually the cross is suspended near the center of the chest). On his right hand is his Episcopal ring, which is unjeweled gold. His left hand holds his breviary. (The rosary, Episcopal cross, ring, and breviary are all in the Neumann Collection at St. Peter's, Philadelphia.)

Although Neumann was a small man (his passport sets his height at about 5 feet 2 inches), the photograph seems to indicate that he had a stocky build, especially around the shoulders. Perhaps this is only an illusion, because he seems to be wearing a thick sweater which appears just above his collar. Today, Redemptorists wear their collars more form-fitting to the neck, and it strikes them as odd that Neumann's collar is so obviously wide. Perhaps the lack of central heating in the Churches and Rectories of that day forced the under-the-habit sweater style upon the priests of the 1850's.

As to John Neumann's ordinary appearance, Michael Curley, C.SS.R., in his definitive work *Venerable John Neumann, C.SS.R.*, states:

> His appearance had none of the commanding features usually associated with great leaders. A rather short man, he was just over five feet, two inches in height, with a body built in proportion, weighing, apparently, in the neighborhood of one hundred and fifty pounds. As a young priest he had a rugged constitution; but the incessant calls he made on his physical resources took their toll, which became noticeable with the advancing years. His deeply set, penetrating eyes could bore through a person at whom he gazed, though he rarely allowed his gaze to linger, especially on a woman.... The bishop had light brown hair, clear but sallow skin, a rather wide mouth, usually firmly set but occasionally breaking into a pleasant and gracious smile.

As a seminarian in Prague, John Neumann began this journal in 1834 and continued it for six years. He wrote at various times in French, German and English. The original is now in the Redemptorist Archives. It provides both an authentic record of his daily life and priceless insight into his spiritual development.

(Archdiocese of Philadelphia)

(Facing page) The stained glass windows depicting Neumann's life are from the Neumann shrine at St. Peter's.

That Christ be formed in Me.

These books, including some of his texts from seminary years, were cherished by Neumann all of his life. Much of his library is still intact in Redemptorist Archives.

(Archdiocese of Philadelphia)

Bishop Neumann's private altar is preserved in shrine on the grounds of Our Lady of Angels College in Glen Riddle, Aston, PA. The original three Sisters of the order of the Sisters of St. Francis, a community founded by Bishop Neumann, professed their vows before this altar.

(Archdiocese of Philadelphia)

The Neumann Chalice

(Archdiocese of Philadelphia)

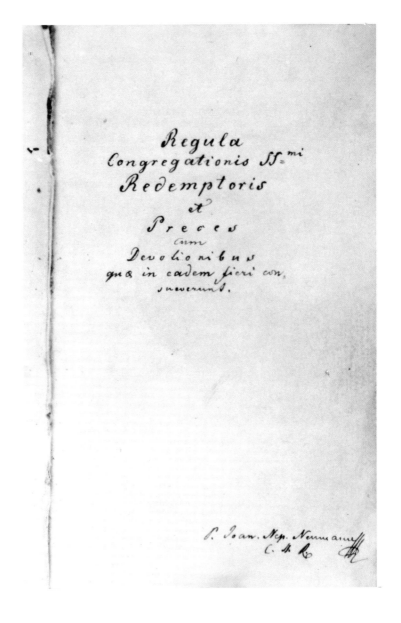

Neumann's autographed copy of the Rule of the Redemptorist Congregation, which he joined in 1840.

First to join Redemptorist Fathers in America.

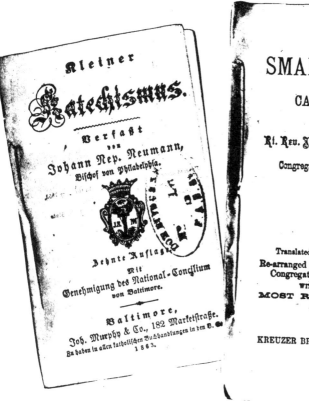

(above): As superior of the Redemptorist Foundation in
Pittsburgh, Neumann found time to write Catechisms, in both
German and English, which were in use among Catholic
children in the United States long after the bishop's death.

(Archdiocese of Philadelphia)

Reading in the south and west. For the most part they were poor and on the lowest rung of the social ladder. Ever so many could not speak English, or they spoke it with an accent; their ways and manners were not American; they tended to live in enclaves. The American Nativists looked upon them with suspicion and hostility. They needed and received special pastoral care from their bishop.

This vast diocese called for a staggering schedule of work. Neumann, obviously, was not one who shrank from work. As will be seen, he worked himself not only to the bone but to an early death. He did have a longing to be a truly apostolic bishop, and that longing was frustrated by the inability of one man to cover that vast territory and do justice to his demanding ideals. This is why Neumann hoped to see the diocese divided. Even when the diocese of Newark was created in 1853, and 9,000 square miles were removed from his jurisdiction, he still had a diocese that extended 160 miles from north to south and 150 miles from east to west. Neumann's theme of these early years is seen in the words: "For my part it is my sincere wish that the diocese might be made as small as possible." After the experience of three years, Neumann acted on his plan. At the Eighth Provincial Council of Baltimore in 1855, he proposed that the diocese be divided and that a new diocese be set up in Pottsville. He also declared his willingness to take the poorer diocese of Pottsville. In a later session a proposal was made to set up a diocese at Wilmington, North Carolina. In his letter to Rome, Neumann spoke of his offer to go to Pottsville and then added: "I would prefer the poorest diocese, namely, Wilmington, North Carolina."

Basically, the move is explained by the reasons already given. Other reasons entered into his decision. Neumann, the foreign-born, did not feel completely at ease in the urbane society of such an important See as Philadelphia. He truly loved mission work out in the country and delighted in the simplicity of country life and people. He was groaning under the financial burden of creating parishes and building churches and schools by the hundreds. To this was added the worry of carrying on the construction of the cathedral begun under his predecessor. Although finances were not his forte, one does not hear that the diocese was on the point of bankruptcy. Actually, the wonder is how he carried on all that building program and found money to keep it going. There was also a certain amount of clerical unrest over some aspects of his regime, but one cannot speak of a general discontent. It was Archbishop Kenrick who suggested that the diocese not be divided, that Neumann remain in Philadelphia where "he shines by his distinguished gifts, his piety, zeal and holiness of life," and that he be given a coadjutor who knew how to handle temporal matters. This was the solution adopted by Rome when in December, 1856, nine cardinals proposed James Frederick Wood as the Coadjutor Bishop.

The coming of Bishop Wood was a help for Neumann and the diocese. Bishop Neumann put him in charge of the finances; he also put him in charge of the ongoing construction of the cathedral. Knowing that Bishop Wood was on hand, Neumann could go out, with peace of mind, on long visitations of the country districts of the diocese. Despite these good points, things were not working out well in Philadelphia. The main difficulty centered around Wood's understanding or misreading of the mind of Rome in appointing him coadjutor to the Bishop of Philadelphia. He thought that Neumann was meant to resign and hand the diocese over to him. Actually, Neumann had proposed to have the diocese divided; he had volunteered to go to a poorer and smaller diocese. Neumann never offered to resign the episcopate; he did not think that he had a valid, canonical reason to do so. In his own words: "To give up the episcopal career never entered my mind."

One can see the tension breaking forth in Neumann's proposal at the Ninth Provincial Council of Baltimore in 1858. He proposed that Philadelphia be divided, that a See be erected at Easton, that he be given the poorer diocese of Easton and that Wood get Philadelphia. Rome's answer was that the matter would be decided at the next national or plenary council. Long before that, Neumann died and Bishop Wood, the coadjutor, automatically became the Bishop of Philadelphia.

Spiritual Growth

It is possible to speak of the style of a bishop as he cares for his diocese. Neumann's style was personal contact. The very morning after his arrival and for many a morning after that, he was out visiting the parishes and institutions of the city, meeting the priests, the sisters and the laity. His pastoral zeal brought him to the prison to visit the Skrupinski brothers. Condemned to be hanged for the murder of a boy, they had refused to make their peace with God. Neumann won them over, and they agreed to see the priest that he sent them shortly before they went to their deaths. There is an eloquent memento of that visit in the Neumann museum at St. Peter's, Philadelphia, the noose and the black mask used in executions, a gift from the Moyamensing Prison.

Neumann himself has left us a rich record of his style of personal contact during his eight years as bishop. This is his *Visitation Record,* a record of his travels through the vast expanse of his diocese. Like St. Paul he was "in journeyings often." Even as early as September of his first year he had visited more than half his diocese. Often he was on the road from six to ten weeks at a time. He covered the populous centers every year, the more remote ones every two years. These were, of course, Canonical Visitations in which he carried out the prescriptions of Canon Law and examined the registers of baptisms, confirmations, marriages and deaths; studied the finances and the legal status of church property and inspected the condition of the church and the cemetery. These journeys were also confirmation tours. He would spare no pains to administer it. Once he traveled the twenty-five steep miles from Bellefonte to the remote outmission at Snow Shoe to administer it to one child. Neumann always stressed the importance of Catholics being well instructed. He always gave two special instructions. If he found someone unprepared, Neumann would himself first instruct the child and then confirm him.

In a special way each stop was a "pastoral visit," a parish renewal with "spiritual exercises for three or four days." Neumann met the priests and the people, celebrated parish Masses and preached. He spent hours hearing confessions, and there were thousands waiting for someone who could speak their language. Neumann's native language was German. He could handle Czech and other cognate languages. He mastered English, French, Italian and Spanish. Neumann came across some Irish (mostly from the West of Ireland) who did not speak English. He set himself to the task of learning enough Gaelic to be able to hear their confessions. The story is told that one woman, on coming out of the confessional, exclaimed in her overflowing happiness: "Thanks be to God, we now have an Irish bishop." In his concern for the sick, the bedridden, the elderly and the infirm who could not get to church, Neumann was an apostle of "Home Masses." On his visitations he carried along a portable altar to be ready to say Mass in their homes and gladden them with the blessings of the sacraments. Not every place he visited was a parish with a church. For groups like this he selected a residence and named someone to gather the people, read the Gospel and other spiritual readings and recite the Rosary. It was a taxing and exhausting schedule. The Eucharistic fast was different in those days. Often it was one o'clock before he had breakfast. Despite the rigors of the work, Neumann loved these visits. He felt at home with the poor and the simple country people. Kenrick could well tell Rome that "he travels throughout the diocese like a shining light and with indefatigable labor promotes the piety of the people."

The visitation tours occasioned projects for the growth of Christian life in the diocese. In 1853 Neumann began the Forty Hours Devotion on the feast of Corpus Christi in the church of St. Philip Neri. The Forty Hours Devotion was known three centuries before Neumann's time. It had been held occasionally in Philadelphia before 1853. What Neumann did was to inaugurate it on a diocesan level. A schedule was made calling for the devotion to be held in designated churches so as to cover the entire year. Neumann gave great edification by the way he joined in these devotions whenever possible. To Neumann the Forty Hours was not merely the pious practice of making visits. To him it was the way of seeing that Catholic life in Philadelphia was rooted in the Eucharist; it was a parish mission on a small scale. It involved deeper instruction in Christian teaching by sermons, the frequentation of the sacraments, Mass and visits.

When Neumann was a diocesan priest of New York, he was greatly impressed by the fervor which the introduction of the Confraternity of Mount Carmel had produced in the parish conducted by the Redemptorist, Father Joseph Prost. As bishop he continued to foster Confraternities as means of developing the spiritual life of the people. We hear of the Confraternity of the Blessed Sacrament (inaugurated by Neumann), of Jesus and Mary, of the Scapular, of the Rosary, of the Immaculate Conception. The Society of St. Vincent de Paul sees love for the poor and the needy as the overflow of one's Christian life. The year before Neumann arrived as bishop, there was one Conference of this Society at St. Joseph's. Neumann encouraged the growth of the Society and when he died there were twelve Conferences in the diocese.

Along with Confraternities, Neumann encouraged Lenten devotions and missions. The Lenten devotions were held twice a week; the first night was devoted to the Stations of the Cross; a sermon and benediction were given on the second. He was delighted to have the Redemptorists and the Jesuits for missions. For the Cathedral mission of 1858, Neumann joined his fellow Redemptorists in the work. Neumann says that during the visitation of the diocese he had the consolation of witnessing the happy fruit produced by missions. His one regret is that "there are not more religious here to conduct them."

Neumann also encouraged the men and women religious in their life of holiness. He also had a deep awareness of the work they were doing for the spiritual buildup of the diocese. He himself became a founder of a new Congregation, the Congregation of the Philadelphia Sisters of the Third Order of St. Francis. He was thinking of a Congregation to care for the sick and orphans. In his *ad limina* visit to the Pope in 1854, Pius IX suggested that he found his own, an Order of St. Francis. Father John Hespelein, a Redemptorist at St. Peter's, was the spiritual director of three women who desired to become a religious community in the Franciscan spirit. On April 9, 1855, Neumann invested Mrs. Anna Bachmann, a widow; Barbara Hall, her sister; and Anna Dorn with their religious habit. A year later they made their vows in the bishop's chapel after he had introduced them to the religious life and given them a rule. Under Neumann they cared for the sick, and then they also took on teaching work.

The bishop was mindful of the growth of his priests in holiness. He pointed out to them the bond between liturgy and holiness. Each year he arranged a retreat for them and a special retreat master. He himself gave the retreat in 1853, and it was a source of joy to him. Because of the link between learning and holiness, he arranged Conferences on theological topics four times a year. He would make it a point to be present. Because the diocese was vast and all could not come to Philadelphia, he had regional meetings set up. Kenrick tells us that there was a close bond between Neumann and his priests and especially between him and those he ordained. He showed concern for them not only in life but also in death. He founded "The Association for Deceased Clergymen." Each priest obliged himself to say two Masses when one of his fellow priests died.

External Expansion

In 1852 the Catholic population of the diocese was 170,000. Despite the fact that the New Jersey territory became part of the diocese of Newark in 1853, the population rose to 175,000. The increase came from births, immigration and conversions. With the years the Catholic population continued to grow. By 1858 the number reached 250,000 and that number remained a constant in the reports and almanacs while Neumann lived.

All this increase called for new churches and parishes. Neumann's eight years saw a phenomenal growth. From his report to Rome in 1854 he had completed six churches begun under Kenrick, rebuilt six others and built thirty. The following year he informed Rome that, with regard to the number of churches, Philadelphia "is larger than any other diocese or archdiocese." That was only the halfway mark in his episcopate. When he died, his era saw almost eighty new churches. Immigration complicated the work, calling for special parishes for those who could not speak English. Most of these were German. However, under Neumann, the first Italian parish was created. At first he gave them the use of the chapel in his residence. Shortly after that he bought them an old Methodist church building and this became the beginning of the parish of St. Mary Magdalen de Pazzi, probably the first Italian National parish.

All these new parishes and churches called for more

priests. He needed many more than the hundred and one diocesan priests that he had in 1852. For the English-speaking
Catholics he was fortunate. Here he was helped with priests
from Ireland or seminarians who would complete their studies
in the seminary of the diocese. His pressing problem was
German-speaking priests. Appeals were sent to Europe. The
response was meager. Neumann soon realized that help from
Europe was not adequate. The Church in the United States
would have to solve its own problems and find home remedies
for its needs. The answer was native vocations. Neumann's
answer to this was to foster vocations from youth on and to
start a Minor or Preparatory Seminary. In 1856 Neumann had
twenty young students at St. Charles' Preparatory Seminary in
Ellicott City, Maryland. He wanted one closer to home, in the
diocese. In September, 1859, he opened his own Minor Seminary at Glen Riddle with a class of twenty-six. He saw the
Major and the Minor Seminary as a unit. He says: "This institution, in connection with our Theological Seminary of St.
Charles Borromeo, will, with the blessing of God and our
cooperation, supply us with pious and learned priests to aid in
the fulfillment of our pastoral duties." What he said proved to
be true down the years.

Meanwhile, Neumann was happy to see the growth in
major seminarians. There were thirty-six in 1852, fifty-eight in
1859. The number of priests grew to one hundred and seventy.
For parochial work he was helped not only by the Augustinians, Jesuits and Redemptorists, but also by two other Orders that came into the diocese in the Neumann years, the
Benedictines who took over the remote parish at Bellefonte
with its many widely scattered missions, and the Conventual
Franciscans who took charge of St. Alphonsus' and acted as
Spiritual Directors for the Congregation of the Philadelphia
Sisters of the Third Order of St. Francis.

In his letters to his sister Joan who joined the Sisters of

Mercy of St. Charles Borromeo in Prague, where she was known as Mother Caroline, Neumann speaks of bringing the Order to Philadelphia where it would conduct a hospital and an orphanage. This never materialized. At his death Neumann had only one hospital, St. Joseph's, that the Sisters of St. Joseph gave over to the Sisters of Charity in 1859. His love for the sick and his visits to the hospital, making the rounds of the patients, is vividly described by Mother St. John Fournier. Although Neumann was unable to add another hospital to the diocese, he had the happiness of seeing the order he founded dedicate itself to the care of the sick by visiting them in their homes. This was the beginning of their later hospital work. He did succeed in adding another home for orphans to the diocese, St. Vincent's, Tacony. This is an overflow of Neumann's love of children; with them he was like a father. This was largely, but not exclusively, for Germans. He was very concerned. about children of immigrants who lost their parents. He was also concerned with saving their Catholic faith and practice by having them raised under Catholic auspices.

Catholic Education

The name of John Neumann will always hold a high place in the history of Catholic education. With his strong conviction about education and religion, he promoted parochial schools with unremitting zeal. As a diocesan priest of New York he established schools in his country missions in the Buffalo area. So important was this work to him that he himself acted as teacher for some months after he had to fire the school teacher because of his misconduct. As a Redemptorist he continued this work. When the School Sisters of Notre Dame arrived here in 1847, he not only helped them to get established, but he was fortunate to get them to take over the schools in the Redemptorist parishes in Baltimore, Buffalo and Philadelphia.

With such a background it is obvious that Neumann would be a zealous promoter of parochial schools. Scarcely was he in his See, when two celebrated meetings took place in April that considered the problem of parochial schools and that set up the diocesan board of education. The bishop was the president of the board that was made up of the pastor and two laymen from each parish. Neumann's drive for parish schools was started. Many things fostered his program. One thinks of the encouragement given to Catholic education by the First Plenary Council (May, 1852). A series of eloquent lectures helped the cause. The zeal of the pastors was a great help. The dedication of the teachers also furthered the work. Neumann always was mindful of "the sacrifice which the good people are willing to make." No one can fail to mention Neumann's own untiring efforts. As a realist he could tell the people: "Whatever difficulties may at first attend, and even obstruct, this most desirable undertaking will be gradually overcome by mutual good will and cooperation."

With Neumann's coming in 1852, schools that were closed were reopened, and new schools began to be built in parish after parish. This work became known far and wide, and James McMaster wrote a glowing report on Philadelphia's "fresh spring." In a letter of 1853, Neumann told his father that the number of children in parochial schools had "increased from five hundred to five thousand." He also told him that before another year had passed, he hoped to have ten thousand. His estimate was not far off the mark. In his report to the Pope in 1854, he stated that he had thirty-four parochial schools with an enrollment of almost nine thousand. All during his years, school after school was erected. Schools were erected in the cities and in the country districts. Furthermore, many a far-flung outpost in Pennsylvania and Delaware could boast of a parochial school. In 1858 Neumann backed the founding of a school for blacks who were gathered in the neighborhood of

St. Joseph's and cared for by the Jesuits, Fathers Barbelin and Lilly. In their gratitude, some of these children made the long walk to St. Peter's to be present at the funeral of the bishop who showed such concern for them.

In promoting schools, Neumann insisted on good buildings and good accommodations. He also was concerned with qualified and capable teachers. Here he was helped by Religious Orders that were in the diocese before he came: the Visitation Sisters (who left in 1852), the Madams of the Sacred Heart, the Sisters of the Good Shepherd, of Charity, of St. Joseph, the School Sisters of Notre Dame and the Christian Brothers. During his years he succeeded in bringing in other Orders: the Sisters of the Holy Cross, of Notre Dame de Namur, the Sisters Servants of the Immaculate Heart. Furthermore, it was not long before his own Order, the Philadelphia Sisters of St. Francis, was engaged in this work. He also introduced the Brothers of the Holy Cross.

In a short survey like this, only a passing mention can be made of Neumann's interest in and encouragement of the work of education in the private academies for girls conducted by various Religious Orders. The same applies to the four Catholic colleges: St. Mary's College in Wilmington, founded by Father Patrick Reilly; St. Joseph's College in St. Joseph's, Susquihanna County, founded by Father Vincent O'Reilly; Villanova College that was conducted by the Augustinians; and St. Joseph's College, the college in the city of Philadelphia that was conducted by the Jesuits.

Mention should also be made of Neumann's work in the field of clerical education. Philadelphia had its own seminary, St. Charles Borromeo. On coming into the diocese, Neumann faced a serious seminary crisis. The seminary was conducted by the Vincentians. In 1852 they decided that they had to give it up because too many of their men were being made bishops, including Father Thaddeus Amat, the Rector of St. Charles'.

Neumann would have liked to get another Religious Order to take care of the seminary, but he was unable. The seminary meant so much to him that, despite his lack of priests, he decided to keep the seminary open and have it conducted by the diocesan clergy; it has remained with them to this day.

As one who received an excellent clerical education, Neumann was anxious to see that his seminarians were properly trained. When not away on visitation, he spent some time there every day, giving instructions in pastoral theology. Despite his need for priests in the ministry, every seminarian had to devote two years to philosophy and four to theology. Neumann introduced courses in Church history, liturgy, chant and sacred eloquence. The students at St. Charles' were fortunate in using the facilities of St. Joseph's College for courses in history and science.

Diocesan Programs and Regulations

The Pastoral Letters of a bishop are a good source for learning about the programs and projects a bishop has for his diocese. The section on education has shown the carrying out of the bishop's plans in the Pastoral on Education. Hardly was Neumann in the diocese when he sent out his first Pastoral Letter and also a circular to the clergy dealing with the building of the cathedral that was begun under Archbishop Kenrick in 1846. He had to champion a cause for which there was no money left when he took over the diocese. Neumann championed the cause, collected money, devised various ways for gathering more money when the funds went low. The progress was very slow and discouraging. Neumann told himself that "what is to last long must be built slowly." He adopted the policy of working on it only when he had money at hand. He also appreciated the plight of the people who were building, paying for and supporting their own parish churches and schools. Before he died, Neumann had the consolation of seeing the exterior completed and the roof finished. The ceremony of placing the golden cross on the dome took place on September 14, 1859.

In 1854 and 1855 Neumann issued two pastorals on Mary and her Immaculate Conception. Neumann gave an explanation of the doctrine—another instance of his desire to have Catholics firmly grounded in their faith. He also encouraged devotion to Mary as part and parcel of life in Christ. Mention has already been made of the fact that Neumann opened a preparatory seminary for youths studying for the priesthood. The Pastoral of 1859 explains to the people what an institution like that is. He stressed the importance of "the parental roof," and admitted that "the guardianship of parents is certainly the best nursery of good Christians." At the same time, he tells them that preparatory seminaries are needed to foster vocations. The youth are trained in learning, live in an atmosphere of prayer where their hearts are prepared for every virtue. Neumann was convinced that vocations could come from the families of the poor. The answer to this was a preparatory seminary in the diocese where their vocations could be fostered and where they could be supported by the diocese. The response of the people was most enthusiastic. That year the collection for the seminary fund was $11,442, an amount that was three times that of the previous years. Neumann's proposal was widely proclaimed and was followed in other dioceses.

Neumann's aims for the diocese are also seen in the legislation of the three synods held in 1853, 1855 and 1857. Here one sees his desire to have Catholics well instructed in their faith. Regulations were laid down regarding the proper instruction for the sacraments of Penance and the Eucharist and Matrimony. In places where there was not a parochial school, the pastors were to introduce the Society of Christian Doctrine. Neumann also arranged to have the Society for the Propaga-

tion of the Faith introduced into the diocese. Steps were taken
for the proper and legal incorporation of church property. In
the future, all deeds were to be made out to the bishop and "his
heirs and assigns of the Roman Catholic Congregation of N.
(name of parish)." The pastors were not to hold church property in their own name. An inventory of all church belongings
was to be kept in each parish. Precision was given to the items
that constituted the revenue that belonged to the church and
not to the pastor. The records of personal belongings and
expenses were to be kept separately. Finally, the Synods show
us the importance of liturgy in Neumann's diocese. Vespers
were to be sung in all the churches of the diocese on Sundays
and holydays. No other pious exercise was to take the place of
Vespers because "the solemn cult of the Church, approved and
in vogue for so many centuries, is to be judged as more pleas-
ing to God." If Vespers could not be sung because of insuffi-
cient numbers, the pastor could have other exercises of piety.
Even in this case the pastor should choose prayers taken from
the liturgy or prayers to which the Pope had attached indul-
gences. Neumann encouraged the participation of the people in
the singing of the Mass. It was under him that the first known
Kyriale or book of chants was published in this country.

The Death of Bishop Neumann,
January 5, 1860

To use his own phrase, Neumann was "a sturdy mountain
boy." That was the phrase that he would always use when
Father Alexander Pax, his friend and co-worker on the Buffalo
missions, would check up on the young priest for working too
hard. In some ways the health of the "sturdy mountain boy"
from Prachatitz was never the same after a three-month bout
with fever in 1840. In his Redemptorist years he did have some
sick spells in Baltimore and Pittsburgh, the result of his driv-

ing schedule. In his years as bishop, 1852 to 1860, he is not known to have had any serious health problem. As a matter of fact, he was constantly on the go, sparing no effort to care for that vast diocese. People marveled at his drive and untiring zeal. They always thought of him as strong and robust, as a man with "an iron constitution."

It could be said that Neumann had not so much an "iron constitution" as a "will of steel." Furthermore, as one of his contemporaries notes, "such labors as he underwent would sooner or later weigh down the strongest constitution." With the dawning of the New Year, 1860, Neumann was not a well man. He himself was aware of it; others noticed it. In a letter of January 4th, dealing with affairs of the Sisters, Servants of the Immaculate Heart, he told Sister Magdalen: "I am not feeling well these last few days; otherwise I might have gone up to see Mother Theresa." Of that same day the Jesuit, Father Edward Sourin, who was Neumann's former Vicar General, tells us: "The last time I visited him, I noticed that he was very unwell. I begged him to let me go and call in the assistance of his physicians. But he answered with a smile and said: 'I will be well enough tomorrow.'" He then goes on to say that Neumann went out the next day and never returned.

At the midday meal of January 5th, Neumann went out of his way to keep the conversation light. He did this to hide the fact that he was not feeling well. Shortly after that, Neumann had a visitor. It was his Redemptorist confrere, Father Anthony Urbanczik. He was stopping over in Philadelphia from Pittsburgh on his way to take part in a mission at the Redemptorist church in New York. At first, Neumann had difficulty recognizing him and focusing on him even though they were close friends. Urbanczik noticed the glassy look in Neumann's eyes. When Urbanczik asked about his health, Neumann mentioned about not feeling well for some days, and he also spoke about having a strange feeling, a feeling he never felt before. Neumann made little of this and spoke of an errand he had to do that would take him out into the fresh air. He assured Urbanczik that the fresh air would do him good.

Neumann had two errands. The first dealt with a deed to some diocesan property that had to be duly registered and notarized. The second was about a chalice and ciborium to be sent to Father Otto Kopf, the Benedictine working at Bellefonte, Pennsylvania. After the first errand Neumann was walking along the north side of Vine Street, going towards Thirteenth Street. Suddenly Neumann collapsed on the steps of the home of the Quayne family. Two men passing by carried him into the house and laid him on the carpet. After a few deep breaths Neumann expired. A priest was summoned who anointed him. Bishop Wood also arrived and found "life already extinct." It was January 5, 1860, about half past three in the afternoon when Bishop John Neumann died at the age of forty-nine. The news of the death spread "like wild fire" with "lightning speed." The people were stunned and shocked. Many would not believe their ears and called at the Redemptorists to ask: Is it true? The following day, Thursday, was the feast of Epiphany and the announcement of his death was made at all the Masses.

Bishop Wood, who automatically became bishop of Philadelphia when Neumann died, made the funeral arrangements. The funeral Mass would take place on Monday morning, January 9th, in St. John's, the procathedral. Neumann's body would then lie in state there all during the day and be buried that evening in one of the outside vaults. Until the services in St. John's, the body would lie in state in the cathedral chapel, the building used for services while the cathedral was being built. One significant change was made. Because Neumann was a Redemptorist and because he often expressed the desire to be buried with his confreres, permission was given them to bury him in their church, St. Peter's. Consequently, after the Mass at

St. John's, the body was brought to St. Peter's on the afternoon of January 9th. The next day after the Mass, again sung by Bishop Wood, the body was interred in the vault in the sanctuary of the lower chapel, where it has remained ever since.

No sooner had Neumann died when the "vox populi," the voice of the people, was heard throughout Philadelphia. The people have a sixth sense for holiness; they recognize a holy person, the genuine article. They proclaim it in ever so many ways; they proclaim it with insistence and persistence until finally the Church authorities introduce a person's Cause for canonization. The voice of the people was heard in the profound sorrow, the stunned disbelief and the repeated requests for assurance that the news of his death was true. It was evidenced in crowds at St. John's and St. Peter's, both outside and inside, in the thousands who filled every inch of space along the streets, on the rooftops and at the windows as the procession made its way to St. John's. It was seen in the thousands who jammed the route to St. Peter's to get another look at their bishop when the funeral plans were changed and they learned that there would be another lying-in-state and burial at St. Peter's. These crowds cannot be explained by the curiosity of people to see the funeral of an important bishop. A contemporary write-up says:

"Did we need any evidence of the appreciation in which the distinguished prelate was held by the laity and clergy, as well as by all who knew him, we have certainly witnessed it in the manner in which they collected together, on the occasion of the funeral obsequies, to do honor to his memory and to attest to the love which they bore him."

The "voice of the people" was manifested in the reverence with which they approached the body, kissed the hand or foot and applied some object to the body to keep it as a memento or relic. It was seen in the votive offerings of flowers that constantly decorated his grave. Another manifestation of the "voice of the people" is seen in the conversion of heart that his death occasioned; for some it was a conversion from sin to virtue; for others it was a conversion to a more fervent practice of the Christian life. A very important aspect of the "voice of the people" is seen in the growth of the Neumann legend. This grew right out of the lives of the people. People began to talk of Neumann from their own experiences. One told this story of Neumann's goodness, generosity, charity, self-sacrifice; one told another story. In this way there emerged a composite picture that portrayed a holy person. "The voice of the people" is heard most of all in the people who came to his tomb to pray, not for him, but to him. They prayed that he would intercede for them with the Lord. People came on their own and they brought the sick and needy. It was not long before there were reports of reputed cures, prayers answered and favors granted. Neumann was buried at St. Peter's on January 10th, 1860. Less than a month later, Father Holzer could say to Father Mauron: "Our church has truly become a pilgrimage church. Indeed, everyone looks upon the deceased bishop as a saint."

The passing of the years did not reduce the enthusiasm of the people for visiting Neumann's tomb. Reports mounted of "cures" and favors granted. The people regarded him as a saint and had no doubt that they were praying at the tomb of a saint. Consequently, with the approval of Rome, the Cause for the beatification and canonization was begun in 1886. These investigations took place in the Archdiocese of Philadelphia (at St. Peter's) and in the diocese of Budweis (at Prachatitz in the Neumann home). These take place under the Bishop, under the Ordinary of the place, and that is why this phase is known as the Ordinary Process. Part of the Philadelphia process was the opening of the tomb and the examination and identification of the body. This was the first in the official exhumations of the body.

In 1896 Pope Leo XIII signed the document that authorized the introduction of the Cause at Rome. This was the beginning of the Apostolic Process. This is the first time that such a process was instituted for a person from the United States of America. Here, the test case, the big hurdle is the decree on the heroicity of virtue, that is, that John Neumann was heroic in the practice of the virtues of faith, hope and charity, and the other virtues. Pope Benedict XV issued the decree on Neumann's heroic virtue in 1921. This is a most important document because it describes so clearly what constitutes heroic virtue. It shows that heroicity of virtue does not call for heroics, for the extraordinary and the spectacular. Benedict XV pointed out that heroic holiness consists in fulfilling, with all their daily difficulties, the duties of one's state in life with faith and fidelity, with constancy and perseverance. In the history of holiness, this is a most consoling document; it encourages everyone to find holiness in his own way of life, and this is why the Pope said that Neumann is not merely a model for men, religious and bishops, but for all: "You are all bound to imitate Venerable Neumann."

For beatification, it is necessary to have two medically authenticated miraculous cures obtained through the intercession of Bishop Neumann. After the Sacred Congregation of Rites passed on two miracles, Pope John XXIII gave his papal approval on February 25, 1963. The first miracle, from 1923, is the cure of Eva Benassi, an eleven-year-old girl from the town of Sassuolo near Milan, Italy. One night death was imminent; during the night all symptoms of peritonitis vanished. The second case, from 1949, involves J. Kent Lenahan, Jr., of Villanova, Pennsylvania. As a result of an automobile accident he was crushed between the car and a utility pole. His skull was crushed, one eye was almost jarred out of its socket, he was bleeding copiously from ears, nose and mouth. His fever rose to 107 degrees and his pulse was 160. His parents applied a portion of Bishop Neumann's cassock. Within a few hours his fever dropped to 100 and his pulse was nearly normal. His injuries were on their way to complete healing. Five weeks after the accident he walked unaided from the hospital. Pope John then issued the *Tuto* Decree, the decree that states that it is now safe to proceed with the beatification. The date set for the beatification was June 23rd. The Pope's sickness and death demanded that it be postponed. Bishop Neumann was beatified by Pope Paul VI on October 13, 1963. Pope Paul observed that God in His goodness had given comfort to the beginning of his pontificate by granting him Blessed John Neumann as his first beatification.

After the beatification, various petitions were sent to Rome to continue the process toward eventual canonization. The Redemptorist Superior General, William Gaudreau, sent one in the name of all Neumann's confreres throughout the world. Cardinal Beran of Prague sent one in the name of all Catholics in Czechoslovakia. Another was sent by Cardinal Döpfner of Munich, who made the request in his own name and in the name of 1,500 priests exiled from Czechoslovakia. Archbishop Krol—now Cardinal—Neumann's successor in Philadelphia, was one of the signers of a petition, including the names of cardinals, archbishops and bishops from all over the world.

Pope Paul VI gave his approval and the case was officially reopened on January 27, 1966 with a view toward canonization. The completed testimony on two alleged miracles was forwarded to Rome. At times, in this last phase, Rome dispenses from the necessity of two miracles. This applied to Neumann's case. The miracle for the canonization centers around Michael Flanagan. In 1962, when he was five years old and living in West Philadelphia, he bruised his shin. Cancer of the bone tissue and marrow developed; later, this spread to the lungs and jaws. After a year of intensive suffering, he was blessed with a relic of Bishop Neumann and within six weeks, all traces of cancer disappeared. This case was sent to Rome from the Philadelphia tribunal in 1971. On December 18, 1975, the medical panel in Rome declared that there was no medical explanation for the case. The Congregation for the Causes of Saints on July 13, 1976, gave its approval to the Cause of Sainthood for Bishop Neumann. At the solemn consistory, held on December 20, 1976, Pope Paul VI announced that the canonization would take place on June 19, 1977.

Abbreviations

Beck, *Goldenes Jubiläum*   Bernhard Beck, C.SS.R., *Goldenes Jubiläum des Wirken der Redemptoristenväter an der St. Philomena Kirche in Pittsburg und Ungegund, Pittsburg,* 1889.

Berger, *Leben*   John Berger, C.SS.R., *Leben und Wirken des hochseligen Johannes Nep. Neumann, C.SS.R., Bischofs von Philadelphia,* NY, 1883.

Berger, *Life*   John Berger, C.SS.R., *Life of Right Rev. John N. Neumann, C.SS.R., Fourth Bishop of Philadelphia,* tr. by Eugene Grimm, C.SS.R., NY, 1884.

Berichte,   Berichte der Leopoldinen-Stiftung im Kaiserthume Oesterreich.

Byrne, *Redemptorist Centenaries*   John Byrne, C.SS.R., *The Redemptorist Centenaries,* Philadelphia, 1932.

Curley, *Neumann*   Michael J. Curley, C.SS.R., *Venerable John Neumann, C.SS.R., Fourth Bishop of Philadelphia,* Washington, D.C., 1952.

Curley, *Provincial Story*   Michael J. Curley, C.SS.R., *The Provincial Story. A History of the Baltimore Province of the Congregation of the Most Holy Redeemer,* NY, 1963.

Hosp, *Prost* Eduard Hosp, C.SS.R., "Leben des Paters Josef Prost (1804-1885) nach seinen eigenen Aufzeichnungen," *Spicilegium Historicum, C.SS.R.*, vol. 11 (1963), pp. 374-432.

Knab, *Prost* Raymond Knab, C.SS.R., "Father Joseph Prost, Pioneer Redemptorist in the United States," *Historical Records and Studies*, vol. 22 (1932), pp, 32-84.

Mullaney, *Four Score Years* Thomas W. Mullaney, C.SS.R., *Four Score Years. A Contribution to the History of the Catholic Germans in Rochester*, Rochester, 1916.

RABB, Redemptorist Archives of the Baltimore Province, Brooklyn, NY.

N., Neumann Section of the Archives.

BP,   Berger Papers.

RP, Rodler Papers.

Sampers, *Neumann* Andreas Sampers, C.SS.R., "Joannes Nepomucenus Neumann Kurze Lebensbeschreibung (Baltimore, 27 März 1852)," *Spicilegium Historicum C.SS.R.*, vol. 11 (1963), pp. 82-104.

Wuest, *Annales* Joseph Wuest, C.SS.R., *Annales Congregationis SS. Redemptoris Provinciae Americanae*, 5 vols. in 9 pts. Ilchester, MD, and Boston, 1888-1924.

Notes to the Introduction

1. 7509 Shore Road, Brooklyn, NY, 11209. The archivist is Brother Barnabas Hipkins, C.SS.R.

2. Wuest, *Annales*, vol. 11, p. 416. See also pp. 98-100.

3. Curley, *Provincial Story,* pp. 104-121.

4. Sampers, *Neumann,* pp. 83-104.

5. *Ibid.* pp. 83-84.

6. *Ibid.* p. 83.

7. Curley, *Neumann,* pp. 29-32; 405, n. 26; 408, n. 31; 494.

8. *Ibid.* pp. 493, 495.

9. *Ibid.* p. 494.

10. Berger, *Leben;* Berger, *Life.*

11. Sampers, *Neumann,* p. 83.

12. Benedict XV, *Decretum approbationis virtutum in causa beatificationis et canonizationis Servi Dei Joannis Nepomuceni Neumann:* Acta Apostolicae Sedis 14 (1922), pp. 23-26. For the Pope's talk, see *L'Osservatore Romano,* Dec. 12, 1921; *Analecta C.SS.R.*, 1 (1922), pp. 15-22.

13. Summaries of the Cause can be found in *Analecta C.SS.R.,* 5 (1926), pp. 194-197; 25 (1963), pp. 198-201.

14. See above, n. 12.

15. Paul VI, *Summa gloria:* Acta Apostolicae Sedis 55 (1963), pp. 905-911. The most detailed write-up of the beatification is found in *Analecta C.SS.R.,* 35 (1963), pp. 193-263.

16. Vatican II, *Lumen gentium;* Acta Apostolicae Sedis, 57 (1965) 56, n. 155; *The Sixteen Documents of Vatican II* (Boston: St. Paul Books & Media). See Alfred C. Rush, C.SS.R., "The Second Vatican Council, 1962-1965, and Bishop Neumann." *Records* 85 (1974), pp. 123-128.

Notes to the Text

1. Abbreviations for Jesus, Mary, Joseph, Alphonsus, Theresa. Because of his high regard for the teaching of St. Theresa of Avila on the spiritual life, St. Alphonsus Liguori used her initial on letters. Many Redemptorists continued the practice and added Alphonsus' initial. Neumann likewise admired Theresa. A great student of languages (see below, n. 49), he studied Spanish and made an anthology from the writings of Theresa. See RABB, N., Data 1834-1835; *Mon Journal,* Dec. 25, 27, 1834; Jan. 9, 12, 1835.

2. Philip, who outlived his son by nine months, died on October 16, 1860. He had the happiness of seeing him when he returned as bishop in 1855. See Berger, *Life,* pp. 397-409; Curley, *Neumann,* pp. 242-244.

3. Many Germans migrated to Bohemia from Bavaria to get out of the routes of armies, e.g., Napoleon's. In 1802, Philip Neumann migrated to Prachatitz, twenty-two miles west of Budweis. See Curley, *Neumann,* pp. 2, 19. For maps, see *National Geographic Atlas of the World* (4 ed. Washington, D.C., 1975), pp. 109, 112-113. Prachatitz is the Germanized spelling; the Czech is Prachatice.

4. Philip married Agnes Lebiš on July 17, 1805. His first wife, Antonia Stratokinskou, died in November, 1804, along with the child to whom she was giving birth. The autobiography will show his mother's great influence on Neumann. Because of the difficulty of mail (see below, n. 135), he only found out about her death (1849) in 1851. See RABB, N., RP, Neumann to his father and sisters, June 10, 1851, Baltimore.

5. Catherine married Matthias Berger who died in 1848. See below (n. 14) for their son, John Berger. At the age of 79 she was a witness at the Ordinary Process of her brother's Cause in the Diocese of Budweis. The meetings were held mostly at the family home from 1886 to 1888. She died June 28, 1889. See Curley, *Neumann,* pp. 2, 403, n. 8; *Analecta, C.SS.R.,* Vol. 5 (1926), pp. 194-195. Vol. 36 (1963), p. 199.

6. Veronica married John Kindla who died in 1850. She will feature importantly in her brother's life. See below, nn. 30, 68.

7. Neumann mistakenly thought that he was born on Good Friday. His baptismal record and all Redemptorist cataloges, manuscript and printed, have March 28, 1811, for his birthday. In 1811 that was the Thursday after *Laetare* Sunday. That year Easter came on April 4. For a copy and photocopy of the certificate, see RABB, N. Neumann Family; A. Reimann, C.SS.R., *Böhmerwaldensohn und Bischof von Philadelphia* (Königstein, 1963), plate 3. See also Curley, *Neumann,* p. 403, n. 1; Sampers, *Neumann,* p. 85, n. 3; Wuest, *Annales,* vol. 1, p. 454.

8. The baptismal certificate makes it clear that the name is Marek. From the manuscript one could think that the reading was Maren. See Sampers, *Neumann,* p. 85, n. 4.

9. B. Szczesnik, "John of Nepomuc, St.," *New Catholic Encyclopedia,* vol. 7 (1967), p. 1063.

10. The "Sisters of Charity" or, more precisely, the Sisters of Mercy of St. Charles Borromeo, were founded at Nancy, Lorraine, in 1626, in connection with the Hospital of St.

Charles Borromeo. See M. Heimbucher, *Die Orden und Kongregationen dee Katholichen Kirche* (2 vols., 3 ed. Paderborn, 1933-1934), vol. 2, pp. 271-274. They have no foundation in the United States. Neumann had hopes of bringing them to Philadelphia to conduct a hospital and a home for orphans. See RABB, N., RP, Neumann to Sister Caroline, Nov. 18, 1852, Philadelphia; Neumann to his father, March 2, 1855, Paris; Neumann to Dichtl, Sept. 16, 1856, Philadelphia; see also RABB, N., Prague Province, Neumann to Sister Caroline, Feb. 12, 1855, Budweis.

11. Joan, who was born in 1814 and is better known as Sister or Mother Caroline, joined the Sisters of Mercy of St. Charles in 1840. We hear more of her in the Rodler Papers and the Berger Papers. On his visit home in 1855, Neumann visited the Motherhouse in Prague where she was Superioress. At the age of 73 she gave testimony at Neumann's Ordinary Process at Budweis in 1886. She died April 22, 1887. See Curley, *Neumann,* pp. 242, 403, n. 8; *Analecta C.SS.R.,* vol. 5 (1926), pp. 194-195; vol. 36 (1963), p. 199. See also RABB, N., RP, Coudenhove to Berger, 1872, Vienna.

12. Louise did not marry. She remained home and took care of her aging father and of the household. When he died, the family home (as the biography brings out later) was given to the Sisters of St. Charles as a convent and orphanage. Louise never joined the order, but lived in the family home with the sisters. Neumann's language here is vague. While still home, Neumann described her as good and innocent, as one who does not know the world. He hoped she would become a nun. See RABB, N., *Mon Journal,* Feb. 4, 1835.

13. Wenceslaus, Neumann's much beloved young brother, was born Sept. 4, 1817. He came to America in 1839 and helped his brother in his parishes in the Buffalo district of New York. Along with his brother he joined the Redemptorists in 1840 and was professed as Brother Wenceslaus on Sept. 8, 1845. In his letters home Neumann speaks of sending the letters he received

on to Wenceslaus and tells them how contented he is. Wenceslaus was not much of a letter writer. Typical is this letter of Neumann to his father, dated Nov. 19, 1853 (RABB, N., RP) in which he says of Wenceslaus who was stationed in Detroit: "I invited him to enclose a note also, but he says he knows nothing new to write about, as there has been no change in his condition for years. Otherwise, he is very well satisfied, and beloved by his confreres." He was one of the fifty-one witnesses who testified at his brother's Ordinary (Philadelphia) Process that was held between 1886 and 1888 in the crypt (Neumann Chapel) at St. Peter's. Already a golden jubilarian, he died at New Orleans on April 10, 1896. See Wuest, *Annales*, vol. 4/2, p. 461; 4/1, p. 152; N. Klein, "Death of Brother Wenceslaus Neumann, C.SS.R.," in P. Geiermanm C.SS.R., *Annals of the St. Louis Province of the Congregation of the Most Holy Redeemer* (St. Louis, 1924), vol. 1, pp. 487-490; RABB, Wenceslaus Neumann. See below, n. 135.

14. John Berger, Neumann's nephew, was born April 12, 1839; came to America in 1857; was professed as a Redemptorist on Oct. 15, 1859; and ordained April 1, 1865. They first met in 1855 on Neumann's home visit. The bishop supervised his education when he came to America and was delighted when he decided to join the Redemptorists. When the fame of Neumann's holiness kept growing, Berger, in 1872, began gathering data for a biography. This was published in 1883 in German and in an English translation in 1884. He died at St. Michael's, Baltimore, on Jan. 13, 1884. See Wuest, Annales, vol. 4/1, p. 151; 4/2, p. 457; Berger, *Life*, pp. 7-8; 397-402. For the accounts of the warm relations between him and his uncle, see RABB, Berger File, Berger to his mother, Jan. 7, 1860, Cumberland; Berger to Sister Caroline, Jan. 8/9, 1860, Cumberland; Berger to his grandfather, mother and Aunt Louise, Jan. 12, 1860, Cumberland.

15. Previously on the occasion of the death of their mother, Neumann and his brother renounced all claims of their inherit-

ance in favor of their father. See RABB, N., RP, Neumann to his father and sisters, June 10, Sept. 10, 1851, Baltimore. The archives contain pictures in the folders, "Birthplace and Vicinity," and "Prachatitz."

16. The school year began in November and went through August.

17. There is a problem with chronology here. Neumann tells us that the grammar school lasted six years. He also says that he began the *Gymnasium* studies in 1823. Either he began his schooling in 1817 or he began it in 1818 and completed it in five years. See Curley, *Neumann*, p. 404, n. 11.

18. The director of the school and the catechist was Father Peter Schmidt. From him we learn that Neumann used to coach others, correct the homework of younger students and that he was singled out to give speeches at school functions. See RABB, N., BP, Peter Schmidt to John Berger, Feb. 27, 1872, Falsching. Other important Berger Papers from Europe are Leonard Zdiarsky to Berger, Feb. 27, 1872, Riegenschlag; John Micko to Catherine Berger, March 26, 1872, Krumau; Adalbert Schmidt to Berger, April 4, 1872, Graz; Anton Laad to Berger, April 11, 1872, Kotoun; Carl Krbecek to Berger through Catherine Berger, 1872. This is referred to as Notes. In later references these can be referred to more briefly. Neumann's father was elected to the Town Council and was in charge of the poor and of the forests. See RABB, N., BP, Peter Schmidt to Berger; Berger, *Life*, p. 18; Curley, *Neumann*, p. 4. In a letter to Neumann's father, Peter Schmidt refers to Neumann as "the then little but exceedingly diligent and good-natured pupil." See RABB, N., Prague Province, Peter Schmidt to Philip Neumann, Oct. 12, 1837, Obermaldau.

19. Love of books is a constant theme in the autobiography. His cousin tells us about his early love for books and the pleasure he found in the special bookcase that his parents had made for him. See RABB, N., BP, Micko to Berger. See also below, n. 89.

20. The bishop, Ernest Constantine Ruzicka, was bishop of Budweis from 1816 to 1845. See Sampers, *Neumann*, p. 92, n. 21.

21. His proficiency in this is seen in his entrance examination for the *Gymnasium* and in his theology studies. See RABB, N., *Gymnasium* 1823-1829; Theology 1831-1835. His catechetical experience with children and adults in every phase of his apostolate prepared him for the small and large catechisms. See RABB, N., Catechisms, Bible History. Mother Caroline says that he was a born catechist. See RABB, N., BP, [Mother Caroline, S.S.N.D.] to [Berger], April 21, 1874, Curley, *Neumann*, pp. 161-162. At the Plenary Council of Baltimore in 1852 he was commissioned to write or select an existing German Catechism. It was his own catechism that was published the following year with the approbation of the Council. See Curley, *Neumann*, pp. 161, 204; M. De Meulemeester, *Bibliographie générale des écrivains Rédemptoristes* (3 vols. Louvain, 1933-1939), vol. 2, p. 95; vol. 3, p. 358. For Neumann, the Council and Rome, see Archives of the Congregation for the Propagation of the Faith, *Acta, Scritture riferite nei Congressi, America Centrale*, 1852-1854, vol. 16, fol. 114rv-115r, Neumann to Cardinal Prefect, June 7, 1852, Philadelphia. The reply was sent July 27.

22. Neumann speaks of the priesthood as too exalted for him and beyond his reach. For indications of a childhood attraction for it as reported by his cousin and student friend, see RABB, N., BP, Micko to Berger; Laad to Berger.

23. The Latin Cross is the one large cross from the forehead to the breast and to both shoulders. For the Bohemian practice of calling this the Latin Cross and for distinguishing between the manner in which the laity and the clergy sign themselves, see Berger, *Life*, p. 24.

24. It is from the Prachatitz catechist that we learn so much of Neumann's parents and of his early talents and goodness, and of his diligence in Latin. The grammar school education and the

coaching by Father Peter Schmidt prepared Neumann for the fine showing he made in the entrance examination for the Budweis *Gymnasium*. See RABB, N., BP, Peter Schmidt to Berger; *Gymnasium* 1823-1829; Prague Province, P. Schmidt to P. Neumann, Oct. 12, 1837, Obermaldau; Berger, *Life*, p. 26.

25. J. Kershner, "Piarists," *New Catholic Encyclopedia*, vol. 11 (1967), p. 344. The Piarists, or Order of Poor Clerics of the Mother of God of the Poor Souls, were founded at Rome in 1597 by St. Joseph Calasantius, a Spanish diocesan priest. The Order was founded to give free education to youth, both rich and poor.

26. The educational crisis of these adolescent years was aggravated by this boarding arrangement. In his fifth year, and thereafter, he took a room by himself. See Berger, *Life*, pp. 26-28.

27. The sign probably indicates $, American dollars. He may have intended to indicate the Austrian gulden. See Sampers, *Neumann*, p. 88, n. e.

28. The examinations at the end of the school year were oral and public. See Curley, *Neumann*, p. 10.

29. Here, there are two topics, the professor and the subjects taught. In editing the manuscript, Sampers had difficulty with the original reading and inserted a word. I, too, experienced a difficulty with the original. At the same time, I am not comfortable with the inserted emendation. The original, with the inserted emendation in brackets, reads: "Sein Nachfolger war ebenso gelehrt und [=wie] strenge." The original would then read: "His successor was just as learned and strict." This cannot be because the previous teacher was not strict, but easygoing. The emendation reads: "His successor was just as learned as strict," i.e., he was both learned and strict. In this interpretation, the qualities of learning and strictness apply completely to the successor. My translation reads: "His successor was just as learned, and [he was] strict." True, I did have to repeat the words "he was" to describe the successor as strict. At the same time, this translation allows for the possibil-

(below): The pectoral cross worn by Bishop Neumann throughout his years in Philadelphia was given to his nearest relative in the city, George Neumann, a first cousin who had emigrated to the United States and settled in Philadelphia. Generations of the family have treasured this cross.

(Archdiocese of Philadelphia)

A bell, purchased by Neumann for use at the preparatory seminary he established at Glen Riddle, is presently used at the Mother house of the Sisters of St. Francis to announce the evening meal.

(Archdiocese of Philadelphia)

The album presented to Neumann by his native village.

(Archdiocese of Philadelphia)

This painting, symbolizing Bishop Neumann's lifelong concern for the education of Catholic school children, was executed by an Italian artist, Giovanni Gagliardi.

(Archdiocese of Philadelphia)

Bishop Neumann himself wrote out schedules for the Forty Hours Devotion at churches of the diocese all year long. This is one of his manuscripts preserved at the Neumann Shrine at St. Peter's.

(Archdiocese of Philadelphia)

Bishop Neumann Advocate of the Forty Hours Devotion

The Oblate Sisters of Providence are befriended by Him.

He encourages the School Sisters of Notre Dame

Bishop Neumann Blesses Mother Francis O.S.F and The Children of St Alphonsus School

Director of the first Sisters of Mercy in America

Welcoming the Immaculate Heart of Mary Nuns to the East

Pope Pius IX advises him to establish Franciscan Nuns of the Third Order

Some years after Bishop Neumann's death, the house in which he died was acquired by St. John's Day Nursery. The room in which he died was then converted into a chapel.

(Archdiocese of Philadelphia)

Painting depicting the miraculous cure of Eva Benassi, an 11-year-old girl from Sassuolo, Italy, in 1923. This was the first miracle through the intercession of Bishop Neumann.

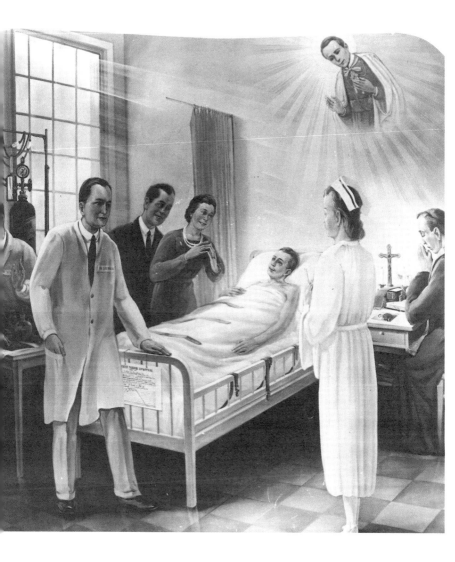

The second miracle through the intercession of Bishop Neumann was the cure of J. Kent Lenahan, Jr., of Villanova, Pennsylvania, in 1949

Bishop Neumann was proclaimed Blessed by Pope Paul VI in 1963 after two miraculous cures attributable to him had been certified by the medical board of the Sacred Congregation to be without scientific explanation. The Beatification took place in the Basilica of St. Peter at the Vatican on October 13, 1963.

(Archdiocese of Philadelphia)

Two workers in St. Peter's Basilica, Vatican City, unfold a huge tapestry depicting Philadelphia Bishop John N. Neumann prior to his beatification ceremony, October 13, 1963. Although a naturalized rather than native American, he was the first American priest to be beatified.

(UPI Photo)

The remains of the body of Bishop Neumann are encased in glass under the main altar in the Shrine in St. Peter's Church in Philadelphia, PA.

ity that Neumann is saying that the previous teacher was learned despite the fact that he was old, easygoing and alcoholic. With regard to the subjects, Latin, religion, mathematics, history and geography were covered in the first four years. The last two were devoted to the Humanities. See RABB, N., *Gymnasium* 1823-1829.

30. This is the celebrated crisis at the end of the fourth year. For the report of the grades, see the archival entry, *Gymnasium* 1823-1829. More detail is given by Berger (*Life*, pp. 27-28) and by Curley (*Neumann*, pp. 11-12). Neumann also tells us about this and the role of his mother and his sister, Veronica. See RABB, N., *Mon Journal*, April 9, 1835.

31. The general idea is that the professor did not manifest completely the spirit of rigid aloofness and distance often associated with the then system of education. Scholastically, under such a teacher, this was the time when Neumann really began to reach his peak. His last two years of the *Gymnasium*, his two years of Philosophy and the first two years of Theology are his years of greatest scholastic achievement and happiness. See the reports in the archival headings: *Gymnasium*, Philosophy, Theology. His enthusiasm for the Humanities is seen in the many anthologies he made of the writings of Vergil, Horace and other classical authors. See RABB, N., Data 1834-1835.

32. During the philosophy years the students also took courses in religion, mathematics, the natural sciences and philology. The transcript shows that Neumann did well. See Philosophy 1829-1831.

33. This was Neumann's study club for discussions on the natural sciences. See RABB, BP, A. Schmidt to Berger; Krbecek Notes.

34. The Budweis Institute of Philosophy was conducted by the Cistercians of the Hohenfurt foundation. Neumann always had warm memories of them and visited them on his visit home in 1855. See Curley, *Neumann*, pp. 15, 244, 454, n. 27. RABB, N., Prague Province, N. to Sister Caroline, Feb. 12, 1855, Budweis.

35. Neumann's interest in the natural sciences goes back to his early childhood and the garden of the catechist, Father Peter Schmidt. By day he studied the flowers; by night, the heavens. See Berger, *Life*, p. 25. Practically all the letters from Neumann's classmates speak of these studies. They also mention the microscope and the telescope that he used so frequently, and the joy he found in introducing others to their secrets. See RABB, N., BP, the letters of A. Schmidt, Zdiarsky, Krbecek. He always kept up his interest in botany. See Curley, *Neumann*, pp. 7, 16, 18, 77, 213. According to De Men-lemeester, he is the author of a lost work on the ferns of North America. See *Bibliographie générale des écrivains Rédemptoristes*, vol. 2, p. 294. The Benedictine Abbot, Boniface Wimmer, tells us that Neumann could identify 400 to 1,000 kinds of plants. See RABB, N., RP, Wimmer to Berger, St. Vincent's Abbey, Westmoreland, PA, March 27, 1872.

36. Neumann was fortunate in getting tutoring from Joseph Jüttner, an artillery commander. See Berger, *Life*, p. 32. He once brought a theorem to the professor who told him he was not able to solve it. Neumann figured it out by himself and proudly showed the answer to his friends and glowingly remarked that the professor once wanted to slap him for his slowness in mathematics. See RABB, N., BP, A. Schmidt to Berger; Krbecek Notes. Neumann spent some lonely hours at his isolated out-mission at Williamsville, working on mathematical problems, and then determined to check himself in such pursuits and work on mathematics only after dinner. See RABB, N., *Mon Journal*, Aug. 30, 31, 1836.

37. See RABB, N., *Mon Journal*, April 9, 1835; Curley, Neumann, pp. 17-18.

38. Neumann put his knowledge of astronomy to good use, both as a diocesan priest of New York and as bishop of Philadelphia. See Curley, *Neumann*, pp. 77, 213-214.

39. See the same sentiment in RABB, N., *Mon Journal*, July 19, 1838.

40. In the talk on the heroicity of Neumann's virtue, Pope Benedict XV speaks of the difficulty that Neumann labored under in not being able to live the regulated life of a seminarian by living in the seminary. See *Analecta* C.SS.R., vol. 1 (1922), p. 17.

41. Neumann's transcript (see below, n. 43) shows that he also studied biblical archaeology.

42. For Josephinism, see below, n. 54. Curley (*Neumann*, pp. 20-21) tells us that the name of this professor was Dr. Francis Linhart. In Neumann's experience this outlook was more prevalent at the University than at the diocesan seminary.

43. In the first year of theology at Budweis, Neumann obtained the highest grades possible in every branch. This played a part in his call to Tonsure and Minor Orders. See RABB, N., Theology 1831-1835.

44. The Scripture professor, Father Charles Koerner, awakened a great love for the Scriptures in Neumann, who was a member of the students' Bible quiz club and had the reputation of always knowing the answers to the questions. The professor's lectures on St. Paul's missionary experiences played a part in Neumann's missionary vocation. See RABB, N., BP, A. Schmidt to Berger, Laad to Berger; Berger, *Life*, pp. 42-44; Curley, *Neumann*, pp. 20-23. In this second year, Neumann also studied philology, pedagogy and Greek.

45. The Leopoldine Society, an Austrian mission society, was founded in 1829 and lasted until 1921. It gave valuable help to the Church in the United States, and published its wellknown *Berichte*. See B. Blied, *Austrian Aid to American Catholics,* 1830-1860, Milwaukee, 1944; T. Roemer, O.F.M., Cap., *Ten Decades of Alms,* St. Louis, 1942. The earliest reports by the pioneer Redemptorists are by S. Sänderl, *Berichte,* Heft 5 (1833), pp. 20-23; 23-28 and by F. Hätscher, *ibid.,* pp. 28-34.

46. Bishop Frederick Baraga, the first bishop of Marquette, was born in Carnolia, a Slovene province, on Jan. 29, 1797, and died Jan. 19, 1868. This celebrated Apostle of the Indians (the

Ottawas and the Chippewas) was inspired by St. Clement Hofbauer, C.SS.R., to do missionary work among the American Indians. The founding of the Leopoldine Society enabled him to realize his ambition. See J. Gregorich, *The Apostle of the Chippewas. The Life Story of the Most Reverend Frederick Baraga,* Lemont, IL, 1932. Neumann's first acquaintance with America came in the talks he heard from Father Peter Schmidt, who recalls Neumann borrowing the book, *Discovery of America.* See RABB, N., BP, P. Schmidt to Berger; Prague Province, P. Schmidt to P. Neumann, Oct. 12, 1837.

47. Neumann regularly spells his good friend's name "Schmid." They were together at the *Gymnasium* at Budweis, but only became close friends about the fourth year. The story of their resolve to do missionary work is told by Schmidt in his letter to Berger, RABB, N., BP. It was a well-guarded secret at that time, even from Neumann's parents. For more on A. Schmidt, see below, n. 70.

48. The Charles University of Prague was founded by Charles IV in 1348. It was called the Charles or Carolinum University. Its name, supervision, organization and aims have undergone many changes in the course of the centuries under various tensions, e.g., German-Czech, Church-State, or under differing ideologies, e.g., Nazism, Communism. See J. Papin, "Charles University of Prague," *New Catholic Encyclopedia*, vol. 3 (1967), p. 509; H. Rashdall, *The Universities of Europe in the Middle Ages,* ed. F. Powicke—A. Emden (3 vols. Oxford 1936, 1969 reprint), vol. 2, pp. 211-234.

49. Neumann was a gifted linguist. Because of his education, he could handle Latin and Greek. His real mother tongue was German. He knew some Czech but later took tutoring lessons from a fellow student to be conversant with this and other Slav languages. He mastered Italian, French, Spanish and English. Later, as a bishop, he mastered enough Gaelic to hear confessions. For a brief account, see Berger, *Life*, pp. 45-48, 340. The reader can look up the many entries under these

languages in the index of M. Curley. Unfortunately, there is no entry under "Spanish." For this, see pp. 29, 51, 163, 408, n. 27, 432, n. 47. So proficient was he in languages that the Austrian government offered him the post of an official secretary. See RABB, N., BP, Laad to Berger. In the Berger papers, practically all the letters from Neumann's classmates mention his knowledge of languages, e.g., Laad, A. Schmidt, Zdiarsky and Krbecek.

50. When the recently-founded Jesuits went to the University of Prague in 1556, they opened an academy near St. Clement's Church. This section of the University was known as the Clementinum; the older section was called the Carolinum. The Clementinum housed the theological students, along with some others. Their classes were held there; the University library was housed there. See J. Papin, *art. cit.,* p. 509.

51. Neumann studied French on his own. At the end of the year he explained to the professor what he had done, asked for an examination and—as he says later on in the autobiography—got "a good school report in French." Neumann soon found out (see below, n. 84) that there was a big difference between a "good school report" and using French in conversation. See RABB, N., BP, Krbecek Notes. After using French in Alsace, Lorraine and France, he tells his parents that he speaks French so well that he speaks it better than Czech. See RABB, N., RP, Neumann to his parents, April 11, 1836, Havre.

52. Neumann bought an English grammar and began to study English privately. He practiced his English on some Englishmen working in a lace factory in Prague, one of whom was a man by the name of Owens from Nottingham. They were delighted to help the young man who wanted to learn their language. In time, he came to write some of his *Journal* in English. See RABB, N., *Mon Journal*, Oct. 24, Dec. 25, 27, 1834; Jan. 9, 12; June 4, 6, 1835. See also the accounts in the Berger Papers written by A. Schmidt, Krbecek and also by Laad who was with him at Prague. He writes his parents from

Havre that he met an Englishman, that it was not hard to speak with him. He happily recounts that the Englishman could not believe that he learned English without a teacher. See RABB, N., RP, Neumann to his parents, April 11, 1836, Havre.

53. The professor of Dogmatic Theology was Dr. Jerome Zeidler, a Premonstratensian. Dr. Stephen Tepaltz, a Cistercian, taught Moral Theology. The professor of Pastoral Theology was Dr. Maximilian Millauer. See Curley, *Neumann*, pp. 26, 27, 33.

54. Josephinism, that takes its name from Emperor Joseph II, 1780-1790, is a system that regulated Church-State relations in Catholic Austria, the Austrian Empire. Absolute State sovereignty called for subordination of the Church to the National State. The Church became a department of the State. This manifests itself in laws affecting Church discipline, worship and organization. Under Joseph II there were so many detailed, picayune regulations that he was caricatured as "Joseph the Sacristan" or "the Sacristan of the Holy Roman Empire." This system has important repercussions in ecclesiology, e.g., the relation of the national Church to the universal Church, of the bishops in the Empire to the universal jurisdiction of the Pope. See F. Maass, "Joseph II, Holy Roman Emperor," *New Catholic Encyclopedia*, vol. 7 (1967), pp. 1113-1114; "Josephinism," *ibid.*, pp. 1118-1119.

55. Under the current ideologies of Josephinism, Febronianism and Gallicanism, there was a tendency to curb Papal prerogatives and to argue against infallibility (not yet a defined doctrine). It was opinions like these that displeased Neumann. To counteract such views in ecclesiology, he delved into the writings of the Fathers of the Church, of Saints Thomas Aquinas, Peter Canisius, Robert Bellarmine, and of the Council of Trent. In this way he grew in the appreciation of theological tradition and grounded his own positions on sound theological sources. Among his many theological treatises, preserved in RABB, there is one written at this time on Papal

infallibility. See RABB, N., BP, A. Schmidt to Berger; Laad to Berger; Seminary Letters, Neumann to Holba, June 7, 1834. Neumann tells us that he was ridiculed by some of the students for his "hyper-orthodoxy." See *Mon Journal*, Dec. 10, 1834. See Berger, *Life*, p. 61; Curley, *Neumann*, p. 27.

56. His *Journal* (July 19, 1835) tells us that he left Prague on the 8th and arrived at Prachatitz on the 10th.

57. This is the canonical examination for priesthood taken at the end of the studies. The account implies that it took place in Prague and not in Budweis. It lasted ten to twelve hours. See RABB, N., *Mon Journal*, July 7, 1835; BP, Laad to Berger; Berger File, A. Schmidt to Berger, April 20, 1883, Graz.

58. Hugh Nolan, *The Most Reverend Francis Patrick Kenrick, Third Bishop of Philadelphia.* 1830-1851, Philadelphia, 1948; John Marschall, C.S.V., "Francis Patrick Kenrick, 1851-1863, The Baltimore Years," Typed Ph.D. dissertation, The Catholic University of America, Washington, D.C., 1965.

59. Father Hermann Dichtl played a very important role in Neumann's life. Neumann kept in touch with him through the years. See Curley, *Neumann*, p. 520, s.v. "Dichtl."

60. J. Guennou, "Paris Foreign Mission Society," *New Catholic Encyclopedia*, vol. 10 (1967), p. 1016. Founded in 1660, this is a religious institute of diocesan priests, the first one devoted exclusively to foreign missions.

61. As a student of theology, Neumann took for granted that he would be ordained at the end of the fourth year. Doubt began to arise early in January. See RABB, N., Seminary Letters, Neumann to his parents, Jan. 1, April 3, 1835, Prague. He had revived hope when those not ordained from the class of 1834 were ordained on May 13, 1835. See RP, Neumann to his parents, May 16, 1835, Prague. Gradually, all hope was lost for other ordinations in Budweis in 1835. Various elements enter into this decision: 1) the age and health of the bishop; 2) many in the previous class had not received ordination or assignments until May, 1835; 3) the superabundance of priests

for the diocese; 4) the telling argument is supplied by Neumann's friend, A. Laad, namely, the refusal of the government to provide a title of support for so many priests. See RABB, N., BP, Laad to Berger; Krbecek Notes. Neumann's *Journal* is filled with entries for June, July and August. Laad tells us that he himself was ordained a year later in 1836.

62. This involves the risk of leaving for America without being ordained and of having no written guarantee of being accepted by an American bishop. It also involves the suffering of leaving before the family had the happiness of seeing him ordained. For his dread of telling the family, and his pain in telling them and seeing their pain, and the suffering of separation with the possibility of never seeing them again, see RABB, N., *Mon Journal*, June 22, 23, 26, 28-29; July 2-7, 21; Dec. 13, 1835. For some excerpts from the *Journal*, see Berger, *Life*, pp. 92-93, 108-109.

63. The brevity of the account raises a difficulty. It seems that the bishop was more against Father Dichtl's plan of setting up a missionary society. See Curley, *Neumann*, p. 39.

64. RABB, N., BP, Krbecek Notes.

65. It was almost mid-December when his friend, Adalbert Schmidt, informed him that the passports had arrived at the bishop's office. See RABB, N., *Mon Journal*, Dec. 13, 1835. Here he also speaks of the pain of separation.

66. On July 20 Neumann told his mother and sisters. She was less astonished and frightened than he thought. She pointed out all the difficulties and, with a mother's insight, intimated understanding. His sisters were disconsolate. He did not tell his father then, but he suspected that he knew. See RABB, N., *Mon Journal*, July 25, 1835. He told his father on the 26th. His sorrow was great and he tried to hide it with a smile. On the 9th of August he received the written consent of his father, a consent that was not given very enthusiastically. The father pointed out the temporal support that Neumann owed him and the family. See *Mon Journal*, July 29, August 9, 21, 1835; Berger, *Life*, pp. 97-99.

67. This was the last pilgrimage made before leaving home. During these months, Neumann had gone on pilgrimages to various shrines, e.g., Nepomuc, Krumau, Gojau, Strakonitz, etc. Berger (*Life*, pp. 95-103) and Curley (*Neumann*, p. 29) list these and other places. They give the Germanized spellings, e.g., Strakonitz=Strakonice. For helpful maps and information, see *National Geographic Atlas of the World* (1975), 109, 112/113; J. Chysky and Others, *Guide to Czechoslovakia*, Prague, 1965; J. Demek-M. Strida, *Geography of Czechoslovakia*, Prague, 1971.

68. The mutual sorrow of separation, perhaps never to see each other again, caused Neumann to leave quietly without saying good-bye. He did this in a letter that he sent three days later from Budweis. Here he tells his parents and family that he wanted to lessen the mutual pain of farewell. See RABB, N., Prague Province, Neumann to his parents, Feb. 11, 1836, Budweis. English translations can be found in Berger, *Life*, pp. 110-111 and Curley, *Neumann*, pp. 41-42. It is not hard to imagine how Neumann could carry that off. His departure on Feb. 8 was like the constant departures of the past months, e.g., pilgrimages and business trips to Budweis. The family knew of his missionary plans. They did not oppose his vocation. However, they did not want to hear talk around the house about his leaving. When his father gave his written consent, he said he never wanted to say good-bye. See RABB, N., *Mon Journal*, Aug. 8, 21, 1835. See also the accounts in the Rodler Papers, Laad to Berger, Krbecek Notes. The only one in on his departure was Veronica. See Curley, *Neumann*, p. 41.

69. The bishop gave his blessing but not the canonical dimissorial letter that would allow Neumann, a cleric of the Diocese of Budweis, to be ordained elsewhere. Probably, the bishop wanted to wait until Neumann had definite news.

70. Schmidt traveled with Neumann as far as the town of Einsiedel. See RABB, N., *Mon Journal*, Feb. 17, 1836. He remained in Europe and became Rector of the Graz seminary.

Neumann visited him there in 1855. See RABB, Berger File, A. Schmidt to Berger, April 20, 1883, Graz. For details of Neumann's travel from Prachatitz to Strassburg, see RABB, N, RP, Neumann to his parents, Feb. 28, 1836, Strassburg. For excerpts, see *Berichte,* vol. 10 (1837), pp. 49-50; Wuest, *Annales,* vol. 1, pp. 255-256.

71. RABB, N., *Mon Journal,* Feb. 17, 20, 1836. Neumann brought letters of recommendation with him from Prachatitz and from every stop on the way. They proved helpful. See the remarks in Neumann's letter (n. 70).

72. Altötting is a very ancient and celebrated Marian shrine that houses the thirteenth century statue of Our Lady of Grace. See M. McCarthy, "Altötting," *New Catholic Encyclopedia,* vol. 1 (1967), p. 355.

73. The Royal *Hartschier* Bodyguard is the Bavarian institution that is rooted in the Middle Ages and which survived until 1918. See Sampers, *Neumann,* p. 93, n. 25. See also, "Hartschier," *Brockhaus Enzyklopädie,* vol. 8 (1969), pp. 202-203; "Leibgarde," *ibid.,* vol. 11 (1970), p. 295.

74. Dr. Phillips was a Professor at the University of Munich, a convert and an ardent promoter of the missions. See Wuest, *Annales,* vol. 1, p. 256; Curley, *Neumann,* p. 45.

75. John Martin Henni, the first bishop (1843) and archbishop (1875) of Milwaukee, was in Europe to obtain financial aid for his diocese of Cincinnati. See P. Johnson, *Crosier on the Frontier: Life of John Martin Henni,* Madison, 1959. Henni's news was devastating. The problem of the dimissorial letter came up again and Henni discouraged Neumann from going on to America without one. See RABB, N., *Mon Journal,* Feb. 20-21, 1836.

76. Bishop Bruté was the first bishop of Vincennes, the present Indianapolis, from 1834 to 1839. His European visit was made to procure help. See J. Tierney, "Bruté De Remur, Simon William Gabriel," *New Catholic Encyclopedia,* vol. 2 (1967), p. 842. As will be seen, nothing materialized from Neumann's

request; his letter never reached him; they never met.

77. Only one sentence covers his stay in Augsburg. To Neumann, Augsburg was a Catholic publishing center, the best city for the purchase of German books, the last outpost for genuine German culture and language because the more one traveled westward into Alsace and Lorraine, so much the more did German deteriorate. See RABB, N., *Mon Journal*, Feb. 27, 1836. See also the letter to his parents of Feb. 28 (above, n. 70).

78. The autobiography is somewhat vague here. In the letter to his parents, sent from Strassburg (above, n. 70), he tells them that he arrived at midnight, Feb. 26.

79. Here in Strassburg, Neumann met Canon Räss, the first in the chain of Europeans involved in his setting out for the United States. A former professor of philosophy (1819) and dogmatic theology (1823) at Mainz, Räss became rector of the Strassburg Seminary (1829), canon of the cathedral (1836), coadjutor (1840), and bishop (1842). He published numerous writings and translations, was a co-founder of the periodical, *Der Katholik* (1821), and died at the age of ninety-three in 1887. See L. Lenhart, "Räss, Andreas," *Lexikon für Theologie und Kirche,* vol. 8 (1963), p. 996. For Neumann, Strassburg was a city of frustrations and disappointments. In a letter to his parents he tells them of the opportunity to practice French, because their bungled German is harder to understand. He then explains that *deutsch* becomes *titish* and *darauf* becomes *druf.* See RABB, N., RP, Neumann to his parents, Feb. 28, 1836, Strassburg.

80. Previously, Henni had brought up the possibility that Neumann might be accepted by New York (*Journal*, Feb. 20, 1836). As will be seen, the letter from Räss to New York will turn out to be very important.

81. The face-to-face meeting of Neumann and Räss is intriguing. Räss, the man who encouraged Neumann to leave Prachatitz, told him that there was no possibility of his going to Philadelphia, that the money set aside for him had been given to others, that he would write to a rich merchant in Paris,

a friend of the missions. In 1852, Neumann's account is very detached. His reaction in 1836 was more emotional. Of Strassburg he says: "No money-here." He tells us that he received nothing from Räss and he then asks: "why?" He complains that Räss consoles him with promises and he goes on to say that Räss does not seem to be informed. He sums up the whole situation by saying that it looks like an underhanded deal, that something underhanded is going on. His German is very expressive: *Ueberhaupt kommt es mir vor als ob eine unbekannte Hand im Spiele wäre.* See RABB, N., *Mon Journal*, March 2-4, 1836; Berger, *Life*, p. 116; *Leben*, p. 115. Later (below, n. 101) Neumann wrote him a very important and informative letter from America.

82. The Sisters gave him a novena booklet in honor of St. Francis Xavier, the Patron Saint of Missions. He received some relics from the chaplain. The chaplain, along with two other priests, admired his zeal, but thought that it was rash to set out "without a written discharge and recommendation from my bishop." See RABB, N., *Mon Journal*, March 7, 1836.

83. This was Father [Albert?] Schaefer. See Curley, *Neumann*, p. 47.

84. For the most part, French was spoken in Nancy. Neumann expected, and did have, some awkward moments. This was a preparation for Paris. See RABB, N., *Mon Journal*, March 5, 7, 1836.

85. *Laetare* Sunday, or the Fourth Sunday of Lent, fell on March 12. See Sampers, *Neumann,* p. 95, n. 28. Neumann stayed in Paris almost a month, from March 12 to April 5. The history of the month can be read in his *Journal.* Generous excerpts in English can be found in Berger, *Life*, pp. 119-134. See Curley, *Neumann*, pp. 47-50. There, one can read of his visits to the churches, of the Holy Week liturgy, differences between the liturgy in Paris and the Roman Ritual. One can see how he was impressed with the piety of the people, rich and poor. He was particularly impressed (*Journal*, March 30) with the Sisters of Charity.

86. C. J. Noonan, "Sulpicians," *New Catholic Encyclopedia*, vol. 13 (1967), p. 785. The Sulpicians founded in 1642 by Father Jean Jacques Olier, take their name from the Paris church of St. Sulpice. Their apostolate is seminary work and training candidates for the priesthood.

87. See above, n. 60.

88. John E. Lynch, C.S.P., "Marriage and Celibacy of the Clergy. The Discipline of the Western Church: An Historico-Canonical Synopsis," *The Jurist,* vol. 32 (1972), p. 211. This was initiated by the Theiner brothers in 1828; an association was formed, mainly in Baden and Württemburg, to work against clerical celibacy. Pope Gregory XVI condemned this movement in his encyclical, *Mirari vos,* of 1832. For the condemnation in the encyclical, see *Acta Sanctae Sedis,* vol. 4 (1868), p. 340.

89. Neumann had cut down on living expenses and eating expenses. His big "temptation" was his love for books. He says: "Before God it is high time to put an end to these purchases," or again: "My greatest temptation is to procure beautiful books." See Berger, *Life,* p. 123; RABB, N., *Mon Journal,* March 22, 1836.

90. The long stay in Paris centered around Bishop Bruté. Neumann was waiting to hear whether he was accepted into the diocese of Vincennes. He also had hopes of waiting in Paris for Bruté and sailing to America with him. By March 25 he knew that Schaefer had been accepted, that three others had not, and that no mention was made of him, a sign that his letter had gone astray. By March 31, Canon Räss was still holding out hope to him. On April 2 he says: "I am filled up with this long delay in Paris." That was Holy Saturday. If no word came by Monday, he decided to leave Tuesday or Wednesday. He is very much concerned about having enough money to make his way to New York. See RABB, N., *Mon Journal,* March 25, 31, April 2, 1836. On Neumann and Bruté, see Berger, *Life,* pp. 130-133; Curley, *Neumann,* pp. 45, 46, 49.

91. Taking off in that unsettled status involved a risk. Nevertheless, the days before sailing saw him optimistic about finding a place. He speaks of New York, Philadelphia, Pittsburgh, Detroit, Vincennes and St. Louis. He also speaks of Germans going to "Louisiana and Albany." See RABB, N., *Mon Journal*, April 1-5, 1836; RP, Neumann to his parents, April 11, 1836, Havre; Wuest, *Annales*, vol. 1, p. 257. See also RP, Neumann to [Dichtl?], June 4, 1837, Cayuga; Curley, *Neumann*, pp. 50, 411, n. 63. Recall the recent good news from Canon Räss (*Journal*, March 31, 1836) that he had written to Bishop Dubois about accepting him for New York.

92. The sentence in German or English is awkward. This is what Neumann says.

93. Details here are confused or omitted. His stagecoach for Rouen and Havre did not leave from St. Germain. To save money, by not having to pay for lodging, he decided to do some traveling by night. Consequently, he walked to Meulan and got a coach there. See RABB, N., *Mon Journal*, April 5, 6, 1836. He also speaks here of his headache, the rudeness of the driver and the growing feeling of loneliness.

94. Havre was the last chance for Neumann to turn back. His letter home and his *Journal* speak of the difficulty of traveling without a friend or acquaintance, of homesickness, of his love and concern for his parents, brother and sisters, and also of his trust in the help of the Lord. See RABB, N., *Mon Journal*, April 6-9, 1836; RP, Neumann to his parents, April 11, 1836, Havre. His *Journal* for the 11th is filled with thoughts about his parents and home.

95. From his *Journal* we know that he arrived in Havre on April 7, 1836. Obviously, the writing of March is a mere slip.

96. This was a bargain price that was a relief for Neumann's financial worries. Originally, the *Europa's* fares were higher. There were two other ships, the *Sully* and the *Troy*, destined for America. The competition brought prices down and Neumann was able to buy a ticket, second class. See RABB, N., *Mon*

Journal, April 9, 1836; Berger, *Life*, pp. 138-139.

97. As already seen, Neumann had some news of this in Paris, but he still hoped. The *Journal*, April 16, 1836, says that the letter from Schaefer "deprives me of almost all hope of Vincennes."

98. The boat was due to leave on April 12. Neumann boarded it the day before and lived on it until it departed on April 20. The delay was due to the Captain who was trying to get more passengers. See Curley, *Neumann*, p. 51. Neumann speaks of sailing out into *Canal la Manche*. Normally this is translated: The Channel or The English Channel. He uses the technical French word, manche, which means a sleeve. This describes the shape of the channel. See "English Channel," *Encyclopedia Britannica, Micropedia,* vol. 3 (1974), p. 899. We know that the boat had to tack for four days in the channel before reaching the open seas. See RABB, N., *Mon Journal*, April 20-24, 1836.

99. In 1836 Trinity Sunday fell on May 29. Neumann shortly goes on to say that they disembarked at New York on Monday, May 30. For a different chronology, see below, n. 101.

100. Aside from the few items he mentions here, the long ocean voyage from April 20 to June 2 is covered in this short paragraph. From his *Journal* we learn how he celebrated the liturgy in spirit on the Rogation Days, Ascension, Pentecost, Trinity Sunday and Corpus Christi. We also learn of his lack of privacy, of the curious onlookers who caused him to write his *Journal* in Latin, of the feeling of awe at the sight of icebergs, of his joy at seeing seaweed that betokened land, and the ecstatic joy of the passengers at seeing America. See RABB, N., *Mon Journal*, April 28, 30; May 11, 22-23, 1836. Here he says that the passengers were "mostly Protestants from the Canton of Berne" in Switzerland. Writing about the passengers in 1836, he tells his father and mother that they were from Alsace, Lorraine, Baden and Switzerland. See RABB, N., RP, Neumann to his parents, April 11, 1836, Havre. Berger, *Life*, pp. 142-149, gives

generous excerpts of entries covering the voyage. In his *Journal* (April 10) he tells us of his delight with the children on board and of his joy in working with them.

101. The 1852 autobiography says: 1) that they anchored at quarantine on Trinity Sunday, May 29, 1836; 2) that they passed over to Long Island in a sloop the following day, May 30; 3) that they went over to New York the same day on the steamship *Columbus*. Accounts from 1836 and 1837 have a different chronology. On Trinity Sunday, May 29, 1836, the ship was anchored about an hour's distance from port. The sick who needed attention and the heavy winds kept them outside the harbor for three more days. Anxious to be in New York for the Thursday morning Mass of Corpus Christi, Neumann kept asking the Captain to be brought ashore. After repeated refusals, the Captain gave in on the seventh request on Thursday, June 2. Neumann was brought to Staten Island. From there he went to New York on the *Hercules* and landed at Manhattan at eleven o'clock. See RABB, N., RP, Neumann to Dean [Endres of Prachatitz], June 27, 1836, New York. The letter can be found in *Berichte*, Heft 10 (1837), pp. 52-55; Wuest, *Annales*, vol. 1, pp. 258-260. See also RABB, N., *Mon Journal*, June 1, 9, 1836. See also Neumann to Räss, May 30, 1837, Cayuga Creek in *Der Katholik*, vol. 66 (1838), pp. 275-280. An English translation can be found in *Central Blatt and Social Justice*, vol. 27 (1934-35), pp. 130-131, 177-178. Neumann's biographers follow the earlier chronology, written when the events were fresh in his mind.

102. For John Dubois, a native of France, an emigré priest from the Revolution, an American citizen, the third bishop of New York from 1826 to 1842, see J. Reynolds, "Dubois, John," *New Catholic Encyclopedia*, vol. 4 (1967), pp. 1079-1080.

103. Neumann was even happier to see Dubois. After landing in New York he spent the whole afternoon walking the streets in pouring rain looking for a Catholic church. Not finding one by evening, he took a room at an inn that was run by a

Swiss. Next morning the innkeeper pointed out the direction to the nearest church. The pastor, Father Schneller, directed him to the cathedral. There he first met Father Raffeiner who brought him to the bishop. See Neumann to Dean Endres, June 27, 1836 (above, n. 101); RABB, N., *Mon Journal*, June 9, 1836.

104. Even though he brought no dimissorials, the bishop was ready to ordain him as a priest for the diocese of New York. The bishop was impressed with the testimonials of his character, conduct and studies. Furthermore, three weeks before Neumann's arrival, Dubois sent a letter to Räss, informing him that Neumann was accepted for New York. Neumann arrived with only one dollar left; he knew nothing about the arrangements regarding his acceptance by New York; he could not presume that the bishop of New York would accept him. It is against this background that we understand Neumann's account in which he tells us that he asked the bishop to lend him money so he could proceed to travel to Michigan and Canada to work among the Indians, that the bishop smiled and told him he would give him money to travel as far as Buffalo and work there as a diocesan priest of New York. See Neumann to Räss, May 30, 1837 (see above, n. 101); Curley, *Neumann*, pp. 55, 412, n. 98. The bishop of Budweis finally sent dimissorials for Neumann on June 28, 1836. The Redemptorist archives in Rome have a certificate dated June 5, 1896. See Sampers, *Neumann,* p. 97, n. 32.

105. For Father Raffeiner and his work among the Germans, see J. Reynolds, "Raffeiner, John Stephen," *New Catholic Encyclopedia*, vol. 12 (1967), p. 64.

106. The ordination took place in "Old St. Patrick's" on Mott Street. In the interests of contemporary style and theology, this sentence has been simplified. We no longer say: "The bishop imparted to me the Holy Order of sub-deacon."

107. Father Raffeiner preached to a packed church. After the Mass, the First Communicants, accompanied by their parents, came up to thank the new priest and each presented him

with a little token of gratitude. See Neumann to Dean Endres (above, n. 101); Wuest, *Annales*, vol. 1, p. 259.

108. Neumann travelled up the Hudson to Albany by boat, from Albany to Schenectady by rail. He then went on to Buffalo, with a stopover in Rochester, via the Erie Canal. The boat, drawn by horses along the bank, made four miles an hour. See Curley, *Neumann*, p. 61.

109. Old St. Joseph's, formerly a Methodist church at the corner of Ely Street and Minerva Road, was bought by the Rochester Germans as their own church in 1835. The Redemptorist, Father Prost, was the first to minister to them here in 1836. New St. Joseph's (destroyed by fire in 1975), the church on Franklin Street, was begun in 1843 and dedicated in 1846. Pictures of both churches can be found in Mullaney, *Four Score Years,* pp. 17, 43. For other works dealing with the early history of the Redemptorists in Rochester, see Wuest, *Annales,* vol. 1, pp. 29, 37-50, 70, 87, 118, 125, 137, 150, 160, 170; Byrne, *Redemptorist Centenaries,* pp. 55, 58, 60-66, 126-140; *Centennial Souvenir,* Rochester, 1936; Knab, Prost, pp. 40, 46, 48-58; J. Galvin, C.SS.R., *The Bells of St. Joseph's:* 1836-1961, Rochester, 1961; Hosp, *Prost,* pp. 388-390. For accounts by diocesan historians, see F. Zwierlein, *The Life and Letters of Bishop McQuaid of Rochester with a History of the Catholic Church, before His Episcopate,* vol. 1 (Rochester, 1925), pp. 71; 79; R. McNamara, *The Diocese of Rochester,* 1868-1968 (Rochester, 1968), pp. 41-43, 76-78, 100-108.

110. Until this time the only Catholic church was St. Patrick's. The pastor, Father Bernard O'Reilly, did his best to care for the Germans. There was a warm bond between him, Neumann and the Redemptorists. Later, as Bishop of Hartford, he was one of the bishops to take part in Neumann's episcopal ordination. See Curley, *Neumann*, pp. 61-63, 177.

111. From his *Journal* we learn about the thrill of his first baptism, the apprehension over his first Sunday sermon, the joy of the people with a priest who knew their language. He

rounded up the children to teach them catechism and was shocked to see that they could not speak correctly either German or English. His first experience showed him the vital necessity for a parish school. See RABB, N., *Mon Journal*, July 5-9, 1836. See also the account in his letter to Räss, above, n. 101.

112. Father Joseph Prost, C.SS.R., was the second Superior of the Redemptorists in the United States, 1835-1841. In October, 1835, while journeying to the Midwest where the first Redemptorists were laboring, he made a brief enforced stay at Rochester because of repair work on the Erie Canal. Here he was welcomed by Father O'Reilly, ministered to the Germans, urged them to get a church and promised to return. On the pleas of the Germans and the invitation of Bishop Dubois, he returned in July, 1836, at the time Neumann was passing through. See Wuest, *Annales*, vol. 1, pp. 29, 37. For more detail and literature, see the following note. For a correction on the first meeting of Prost and Neumann, see below, n. 123.

113. As the autobiography shows, Prost plays an important part in Neumann's life. For literature, see Wuest, *Annales*, vol. 1, pp. 29, 37-50, 95-109; Knab, *Prost,* pp. 32-84; Curley, *Provincial Story,* pp. 33-57, 495, s.v. "Prost"; Hosp, *Prost,* pp. 374-432. In particular, attention should be called to Prost's own account, "Die Geschichte der Gründung unserer Congregationen in den Vereinigten Staaten von Nordamerika von Jahre 1832 bis zum Anfang des Jahres 1843," in Wuest, *Annales*, *Supplementum,* Pt. 1, pp. 1-238. This is also called "Relationes Patris Prost." Hereinafter it will be referred to as "Geschichte." At the end of the preface he tells us that he wrote it at Mautern (Austria) in January, 1857. He writes, *Jänner*, the Austrian dialect for *Januar.* See also Prost to the Leopoldine Foundation, Nov. 12, 1835, Detroit, in *Berichte,* Heft 9 (1836), pp. 63-67.

114. The pioneer priest among the Buffalo Germans was Father John Nicholas Mertz, a native of the diocese of Luxem-

burg (1765). From 1805 he worked in Pennsylvania, Maryland and lastly in the neighborhood of Buffalo, New York. The first church, dedicated to the Lamb of God, was built by him. See Berger, *Life*, pp. 159-161; John Timon, C.M., *Missions in Western New York and Church History of the Diocese of Buffalo* (Buffalo, 1862), pp. 213-215.

115. Father Alexander Pax, born in Metz in 1799, came to Buffalo in 1835 to help Father Mertz. He saw the building of St. Louis Church. Pax and Neumann became close associates. See Curley, *Neumann*, pp. 61, 65. For the letter of Pax see below, n. 119.

116. Pax was delighted to meet a much-needed helper. He offered Neumann the choice of working in the city or in the country. Neumann thought it fitting to choose the country missions because he was ordained on the "Title of the Missions." See Neumann to Räss, May 30, 1837, Cayuga Creek (above, n. 101).

117. In an 1839 letter Neumann speaks of North Bush, Williamsville, [Lancaster] on Cayuga Creek, Pendleton, Shelden, Batavia and Rochester. See RABB, N., RP, Neumann to Dichtl, May 31, 1839, Tonawanda; *Berichte,* Heft 13 (1840), pp. 63-68; Wuest, *Annales*, vol. 1, p. 280. In listing places where Neumann worked, the approximate mileage and direction are given in parentheses. Where Gazetteers differ in mileage, their differences will be indicated. Unless otherwise noted, the point of departure for mileage and direction is Buffalo. In Erie County, Neumann worked in North Bush, now Kenmore (6N), Williamsville (4/8 NE), Lancaster (8/10 E), Swormville, Tonawanda (7/10 N.), and Transit, the railroad name for the post-hamlet of East Amherst (9 1/2 miles East of Tonawanda), Eden (18 1/2 S). In Niagara County, Neumann worked in Pendleton (18 NNE) and Niagara Falls (20 NNW). In Wyoming County, Neumann cared for Shelden (30 ESE); in Genesee County for Batavia (36 EN), and in Monroe County for Rochester (65/70 ENE). The centenary edition of the *Catholic Union*

and Times, June 28, 1931, has interesting write-ups of Neumann's work in many of these places. See also Byrne, *Redemptorist Centenaries,* pp. 293-295. For help in locating these places and ascertaining the approximate mileage from Buffalo, see *National Geographic Atlas of the World* (1975), 29, 6OC; *Commercial Atlas and Marketing Guide* (Rand McNally Co., Chicago, 1974), 376; *Lippincotts New Gazetteer. A Complete Pronouncing Gazetteer or Geographical Dictionary of the World,* ed. A. Heilprin—L. Heilprin, Philadelphia, 1911; *The Columbia Lippincott Gazetteer of the World,* ed. L. Seltzer, New York, 1962; *The Times Index Gazetteer of the World,* London: Times Publishing Co. Ltd., 1965. In the course of time some of these places have become large Catholic centers. It is interesting to see that some of them, e.g., Pendleton, Shelden, Swormville, have still only one parish church. See *The Official Catholic Directory, Anno* 1975, pp. 139-142.

118. The problem was alcohol. George Pax, the nephew of Father Alexander Pax, informs us that this was a problem with school teachers in the loneliness of the country. See RABB, N., BP, G. Pax to Berger, Feb. 16, 1872, Williamsville. The taking over of the task of teaching school shows how important schools were to Neumann. As bishop, he not only strove to have a school in each parish, but he also inaugurated the first Central Board of Education on a diocesan level. See Curley, *Neumann*, pp. 207-212, 263-265.

119. Father Pax was Neumann's advisor, confidant, confessor and friend. As Pax says, he and Neumann were "one in heart and soul." See the letter of Pax on Neumann, dated March 9, 1872, that appeared in the Buffalo paper, *Christliche Woche,* March 31, 1876; Byrne, *Redemptorist Centenaries*, p. 297.

120. From his various missions Neumann was supposed to receive $400.00 a year. He himself tells us that he scarcely received a third of that. See RABB, N., RP, Neumann to Räss, May 30, 1837, Cayuga Creek. See Prost's remarks on Neumann's poverty in "Geschichte," in Wuest, *Annales,*

Supplementum, Pt. 1, p. 122.

121. In Williamsville, Neumann lived in the home of the Trustee, Jacob Wirtz. This was above a tavern. To get to his part of the house, Neumann had to pass through the quarters of the servant girl. Another Trustee, Paul Mueller, jealous that Neumann was not living at his house, started a whispering campaign. Through friends in North Bush, Neumann heard about this. Some of the Trustees held a meeting in the tavern to get Wirtz to get rid of one or the other. Neumann was called down and told what they were discussing. He quietly listened, denied any impropriety and moved to North Bush. His reputation remained intact; the calumniator lost out. See RABB, N., BP, Theodore Noethen Report. Father Noethen (from Cologne) worked in Neumann's missions from 1842 to 1845. See also George Pax (nephew of Father Alexander Pax) to Berger, Feb. 16, 1872, Williamsville; Berger, *Life,* pp. 185-186; Curley, *Neumann,* pp. 70-71. For Father Noethen, see *Christliche Woche,* April 18, 1879.

122. In North Bush Neumann lived in the home of John Schmidt, a native of Lorraine. In a letter home Neumann tells his parents that Schmidt gave him room and board free in view of the reward in the next life. Neumann's letters to the family are warm and newsy, filled with all sorts of detail about life in America. See RABB, N., RP, Neumann to his parents, Sept. 5, 1837, North Bush. The text can be found in *Berichte,* Heft 11 (1838), pp. 56-62; *Der Katholik,* vol. 69 (1838), pp. 61-67; Wuest, *Annales,* vol. 1, pp. 262-267; *Central Blatt and Social Justice,* vol. 17 (1924-25), pp. 163-164, 179-180. In his report to Berger (n. 121), Father Noethen of Cologne tells us that the people in Neumann's missions were mainly from Alsace and Lorraine, that they were not a happy lot and that there was friction between the Alsatians and those from Lorraine. Those in Williamsville were mainly from Alsace; those in North Bush from Lorraine. At the time of the whispering campaign against Neumann, it was the Lorrainers in North Bush who

told him about it and invited him to live with them. Ultimately, they built him a house for himself.

123. J. G. Shea, *A History of the Catholic Church within the Limits of the United States,* vol. 3 (New York, 1890), p. 515; Prost, "Geschichte," in Wuest, *Annales, Supplementum,* Pt. 1, pp. 120-121. Curiously, in his 1857 "Geschichte" (p. 122), Prost overlooks the fact that he first met Neumann in 1836 when he stopped off at Rochester on his way to his Buffalo missions. Here he says that he first made Neumann's acquaintance on the episcopal visitation in 1837.

124. As the next note will show, it is possible that Neumann is confusing 1837 and 1838. In 1837 the bishop wanted Raffeiner to go to Rochester. Prost and the Redemptorists would then take over St. Nicholas', N..Y. They would also conduct the diocesan seminary. Brother Joseph Reisach, who was returning to Europe, was to bring these matters to the Superiors in Vienna. The request was refused because the administration of seminaries and colleges was not in keeping with the Congregation's purpose. See Joseph Reisach, "Relatio," in Wuest, *Annales, Supplementum,* Pt. 1, pp. 306-307. Dubois also brought the matter up in 1835. See Curley, *Provincial Story,* pp. 39-40.

125. Of the three German centers, Rochester, Buffalo and New York City, the most flourishing parish, both spiritually and financially, was Rochester. In 1838, Prost proposed that Pax take over Rochester, that Neumann be assigned to New York because a second priest was needed there, and that the Redemptorists take over Buffalo along with Neumann's missions. His reason was this: Since 1832 the Redemptorists had been trying to establish a foundation where they could live together as a community. The parish of Buffalo, with its surrounding missions, seemed to be the answer. In April or May he went to New York to take the matter up with the bishop. Bishop Dubois was suffering from a stroke. The coadjutor, Bishop Hughes, could not act upon the matter because he had

not yet been named Administrator. Prost claims that he then favored the plan. See Prost, "Geschichte," in Wuest, *Annales, Supplementum,* Pt. 1, pp. 130-132; Knab, *Prost,* pp. 58-59; Curley, *Provincial Story,* p. 48.

126. Father Prost's departure cannot be told quite so simply. He was trying to get a foundation that was free of Trustee trouble and that was suitable for a religious community. He suggested that the new church, that was needed, be built on the Franklin Street property that he purchased in his own name. The Trustees objected. Hoping to bring the people to their senses, he decided to leave Rochester and join the other Redemptorists in Ohio who then thought that there was the possibility of a foundation for a religious community. Prost left in May. See Wuest, *Annales,* vol. 1, pp. 49-50; Mullaney, *Four Score Years,* pp. 28-29; Knab, *Prost,* pp. 58-59. The Germans in Rochester were not abandoned; the next two notes will complete the story.

127. Father Francis Hätscher, one of the Redemptorist pioneers who came to the United States in 1832, was visiting Father Prost before returning to Europe. Father Peter Czackert was also in Rochester for reasons of health. After Prost left, he stayed on at Rochester until August. See Prost, "Geschichte," in Wuest, *Annales, Supplementum,* Pt. 1, pp. 109, 132-133; Wuest, *Annales,* vol. 1, pp. 43, 50, n. 1; Hosp, *Prost,* p. 390.

128. The Germans in Rochester could go to St. Patrick's. Also, every Saturday Father O'Reilly said Mass at St. Joseph's for the Confraternity of Mt. Carmel. Furthermore, Neumann came over from Rochester every two or three months for a year. See Wuest, *Annales,* vol. 1, p. 50; Byrne, *Redemptorist Centenaries,* p. 66; Hosp, *Prost,* p. 390.

129. The best account of the Confraternity and other means used to enkindle the fervor of the people is given by Prost himself in "Geschichte," in Wuest, *Supplementum,* Pt. 1, pp. 107-108. Generous excerpts are found in Mullaney, *Four Score Years,* pp. 18-20.

130. Shortly after making trips to Rochester, Neumann wrote to Prost and spoke glowingly of the fervor of the faithful, their devotion to the Eucharist and to the Scapular. He pleaded with him to return or send another Redemptorist. He also wanted information about introducing the Confraternity of Mt. Carmel into his own parishes. The letter in English can be found in Berger, *Life,* pp. 217-218. The German text (Berger, *Leben,* p. 199; Hosp, *Prost,* p. 397) is taken from the Domestic Chronicles of the Redemptorist House at Puchheim (Austrian Province). This foundation in the diocese of Linz was begun in 1851. The first volume of the Chronicles, almost completely written by Prost, contains inserts dealing with Prost's own life. As is clear, this correspondence had to take place between August, 1838, and August, 1839.

131. For the Redemptorist faculty to bless the Scapular of the Blessed Virgin Mary of Mt. Carmel, see *Documenta authentica facultatum et gratiarum spiritualium quas Congregationi SS. Redemptoris S. Sedes concessit* (Regensburg, 1903), p. 161.

132. This is part of the verse of Ecclesiastes 4:10: "If one should fall, the other helps him up; but woe to the man by himself with no one to help him when he falls down." Neumann asked Prost for advice; Prost's advice was: Live in community.

133. As an eloquent speaker, Lutgen succeeded in winning some over to him. The importance of the situation is seen in the fact that the three priests, Pax, Mertz and Neumann, came together in Williamsville and pointed out to the people the need of obeying the orders of the bishop. See RABB, N., BP, G. Pax to Berger, Feb. 13, 1872; Berger, *Life,* pp. 177-179; Curley, *Neumann,* pp. 75-76. Curley spells the name "Lutsche."

134. His nephew (Berger, *Life,* p. 179) gives warm anecdotes about Neumann's house. Father Pax tells us how poor a cook he was in not preparing cooked food to take care of himself properly. See *Christliche Woche,* March 31, 1876; Byrne, *Redemptorist Centenaries,* p. 296. Neumann's joy was a house

next to the church and so close to the Blessed Sacrament.

135. The two brothers met not in 1838, but on Sept. 25, 1839. Neumann invited his brother to join him in America and sent helpful hints and instructions about travel. He was delighted when his parents made the sacrifice of letting their youngest leave for America. Wenceslaus brought news from home, the first direct news Neumann received since he left Prachatitz. His letters to Europe got through; letters from home until then did not get through to him. Wenceslaus took care of the house, the church buildings and schools, did carpentry work, taught school and catechism. With Wenceslaus, Neumann had companionship and he also had a warm welcome awaiting him when he returned from a missionary journey. See RABB, N., RP, Neumann to his parents, Oct. 7, 1838, Tonawanda; Oct. 4, 1839, North Bush. Generous excerpts of the second letter are given by Berger, *Life*, pp. 180-181. For Wenceslaus' work in teaching school see RABB, N., Letters 1839, Neumann to a friend, Dec. 12, Dec. 19, 1839, Tonawanda.

136. Shelden, 30 miles ESE of Buffalo, is also mentioned in Neumann's letter to Dichtl in which he speaks of the need of more priests for the work in America. See RABB, N., RP, Neumann to Dichtl, May 31, 1839, Tonawanda; Wuest, *Annales*, vol. 1, p. 280. For more details on geography, see above, n. 117.

137. With the Pittsburgh foundation in 1839 (see below, n. 144), the Redemptorists had a place where they could live together as a community. Father Sänderl, one of the original pioneers, was not called by Prost to join the first community. Because there was still hope that Rochester would be the second foundation, he went there in 1839 and the Redemptorists have been there since. See Prost, "Geschichte," in Wuest, *Annales, Supplementum,* Pt. 1, pp. 133, 167; Wuest, *Annales*, vol. 1, pp. 66, 70-71; Hosp, *Prost,* p. 393.

138. Neumann to use his own phrase—was "a sturdy

mountain boy." His nephew tells us (*Life,* p. 216) that this three-month spell of fever in 1840 marks the beginning in the decline of his robust health. See the interesting remarks in the letter of Father Pax as found in *Christliche Woche,* March 31, 1876; Byrne, *Redemptorist Centenaries,* pp. 296-297.

139. He would not stay over the weekend because he wanted to get back for confessions and Sunday Masses. See Berger, *Life*, p. 216.

140. *Concilia Provincialia Baltimori habita ab anno* 1829 *usque ad annum* 1849 (2 ed. Baltimore, 1851), p. 163; Knab, *Prost*, pp. 66-67. The Council was held in May. Actually, Prost returned to Pittsburgh for a while, but was back in Baltimore at the end of July. See Prost, "Geschichte" in Wuest, *Annales, Supplementum,* Pt. 1, pp. 181, 186.

141. Berger, *Life*, pp. 219-220; Curley, *Neumann*, pp. 79-80.

142. Only two knew of Neumann's resolve, his brother Wenceslaus, who decided to join him, and his confessor, Father Pax, who was encouraging him to become a Redemptorist. On the advice of Pax and Prost, Neumann departed and left things in their hands. Bishop Hughes acquiesced when won over by Prost. See Prost, "Geschichte," in Wuest, *Supplementum*, Pt. 1, p. 198; RABB, N., RP, Wenceslaus to his parents, Neumann to his parents, May 12, 1841, Pittsburgh.

143. Dunkirk, N.Y., ca. midway between Buffalo and Erie, Pennsylvania.

144. In 1839, after seven frustrating years, the Redemptorists under Father Prost succeeded in getting this foundation at Pittsburgh where they could live together as a religious community. See Wuest, *Annales*, vol. 1, pp. 56-70; Byrne, *Redemptorist Centenaries,* pp. 75-76, 80-83.

145. The Germans were divided into two factions. Some wanted to use the "Factory Church," a former cotton factory. Others wanted to use St. Patrick's, the old "Irish Church," when the congregation moved to the new and bigger St. Paul's. With the coming of Prost the "Factory Church" was chosen,

and this became St Philomena's. See Prost, "Geschichte," in Wuest, *Supplementum,* Pt. 1, pp. 141, 146-167; Beck, Goldenes Jubiläum, pp. 96-120; Knab, *Prost,* pp. 62-66. Beck, on p. 112, furnishes a drawing of the "Factory Church."

146. These stations were Butler, Pine Creek, Wexford, McKeesport, Perryville and Williamsport. Byrne (*Redemptorist Centenaries,* pp. 85-92) gives write-ups of these and other centers. See also Beck, *Goldenes Jubiläum,* p. 122.

147. The first one to receive the habit was Brother Joseph Reisach, a native of Innsbruck who was accepted in Europe and then came to the United States where he was invested in 1835. See RABB, *The Province Story,* vol. I (May 1, 1975), p. 13. Prost explains that they wanted to have Neumann's investiture as solemn as possible, but that they could not use the prescribed prayers and ceremonies because the book, along with other things, was destroyed in a fire in New York. They got together and recalled as much as they could. See Prost, "Geschichte," in Wuest, *Annales, Supplementum,* Pt. 1, p. 199. Prost's memory fails him here when he puts the investiture shortly after New Year, 1841.

148. Some years later, in a letter to his nephew, Neumann pointed out his difficulty as a novice when the Congregation did not have someone designated as Novice Master or a set place for the novitiate. See RABB, N., Letters 1858, Neumann to John Berger, Sept. 13, 1858, Philadelphia.

149. These were the spiritual exercises prescribed by the rule for professed Redemptorists. The novice rule called for more. Some years later Neumann got a copy and translated it from Italian into German. See Curley, *Neumann,* p. 90. Neumann's translation is in RABB.

150. Father Alexander Czvitkovicz, regularly called Father Alexander, was the Superior of the United States Redemptorists from 1841 to 1845. See Curley, *Provincial Story,* pp. 58-82. See also his own Memoirs and diary in Wuest, *Annales,* vol. 1, pp. 287-296; *Supplementum,* Pt. 1, pp. 372-454.

151. The title, *Frater*, is used by the Redemptorists to designate a clerical novice and student, one studying for the priesthood.

152. On May 24, 1841, Father Alexander deposed Father Prost as the Pittsburgh Superior. Later, on Nov. 25, he uncanonically expelled him from the Congregation. The saintly Father Joseph Passerat, the Superior in Vienna to whom the American Redemptorists were then subject, annulled the decision. For this sad story, see Wuest, *Annales*, vol. 1, pp. 97-109; Knab, *Prost,* pp. 70-83; Curley, *Provincial Story,* pp. 64-67; Hosp, *Prost*, pp. 397-399. The writings of both men in Wuest, *Supplementum,* and the remarks of Wuest are most informative.

153. Bishop Edward Fenwick, O.P., of Cincinnati, sent his Vicar General, Frederick Résé (later bishop of Detroit), to Europe to seek financial help and personnel. Résé's request to Fr. Joseph Passerat, the Superior of the Transalpine Redemptorists, resulted in six Redemptorists leaving for the United States. These pioneers first worked in Ohio and in Michigan and Wisconsin. At that time they did not succeed in establishing a foundation where the Redemptorists could live as a religious community. See Byrne, *Redemptorist Centenaries*, pp. 41-79; Curley, *Provincial Story,* pp. 1-32.

154. Brother Louis Kenning was the first to ask to join the Redemptorists in the United States. He came here from Hanover, Germany, with his mother, three brothers and sister in 1834. Prost accepted him on Nov. 12, 1836. He received the habit at Pittsburgh on Feb. 2, 1840, and was professed at Baltimore (Old St. James) on Dec. 14, 1843. He died at New Orleans on April 6, 1875. See Wuest, *Annales*, vol. 1, p. 458; Knab, *Prost,* p. 52; RABB, *The Province Story,* vol. 1 (May 1, 1975), pp. 11-12. See the interesting history and laudatory accounts in Prost to F. Röder June 10, 1875, Puchheim (Austria) in Wuest, *Annales, Supplementum*, Pt. 1, pp. 233-238.

155. Pax tells us what a source of help and comfort

Neumann was. See *Christliche Woche*, March 31, 1876; Byrne, *Redemptorist Centenaries*, p. 297.

156. In 1841 Hughes was not only Coadjutor with the right of succession, but he was also the Apostolic Administrator of the diocese. See F. Cohalon, "Hughes, John Joseph," *New Catholic Encyclopedia*, vol. 7 (1967), p. 197. The Redemptorists had worked in Buffalo since 1837. Their first foundation there goes back to 1844. See Byrne, *Redemptorist Centenaries,* pp. 221-227; RABB, Msgr. J. Keitz, C.SS.R., "History of St. Mary's Church, Buffalo, New York."

157. Two days after Neumann left for Ohio, Prost wrote him a letter. Consider all the orders Neumann received to go here and there since he first joined the Redemptorists at Pittsburgh. Furthermore, the first Redemptorist Neumann ever met was Prost; he felt close to him. He now saw him deposed from his Superiorship at Pittsburgh by Alexander. He saw personality conflicts in men in command. It was a crisis for Neumann. Prost sent him a very warm letter of encouragement, urged him to live with human failings and extolled the blessings of obedience. See RABB, N. Data 1841, Prost to Neumann, Sept.18, 1841, Rochester.

158. It may well be that Tschenhens suspected that Neumann's vocation was in jeopardy and urged Alexander to call Neumann to Baltimore where the novice could get some quiet and solitude. See Curley, *Neumann*, p. 91; Wuest, *Annales, Supplementum*, Pt. 1, p. 254.

159. The name of the town is missing.

160. John Baptist Purcell succeeded Fenwick as bishop of Cincinnati in 1833 and became its first archbishop in 1850. See M. Carthy, "Purcell, John Baptist." *New Catholic Encyclopedia*, vol. 11 (1967), pp. 1029-1030.

161. One has only to recall the trials and setbacks of the early years and the difficulties in getting a permanent foundation for a religious community. The rumor had it that the Redemptorists were giving up and returning to Europe. See Wuest, *Annales*, vol. 4/1, p. 141.

162. Canton, Ohio, is 20 miles SSE of Akron. Randolph, further north and east, is 10 miles south of Ravenna. See *Rand McNally Road Atlas* (51 ed. Chicago, 1975), 80/81.

163. This is from the months of Neumann's stay in Pittsburgh as a novice. At the request of Archbishop Eccleston the Redemptorists paid visits to Wheeling, West Virginia, and the surrounding area. From there they went to Steubenville, Ohio. See Beck, *Goldenes Jubiläum*, pp. 122, 334; Byrne, *Redemptorist Centenaries,* p. 90. See also E. Schmitz, "Eccleston, Samuel," *New Catholic Encyclopedia,* vol. 5 (1967), p. 35.

164. The Baltimore and Ohio Railroad, that opened its first thirteen miles of track between Baltimore and Ellicott's Mills (Ellicott City) on May 24, 1830, got to Wheeling only in 1852. See T. Shedd, "Railroads and Locomotives," *Encyclopedia Britannica, Macropedia,* vol. 15 (1974), p. 480.

165. In the days of Father Prost, the pastor of St. John's Church in Baltimore, Father Benedict Bayer, was anxious to have the Redemptorists take over the church and care of the Germans. Archbishop Eccleston arranged this on the condition that the Redemptorists take charge of the Germans there and in the whole diocese, that they build a larger church on the same site as the old one (Saratoga Street and Park Avenue) and that they build a school for the Germans. This dates back to July 26, 1840. While St. John's was being destroyed to make room for St. Alphonsus', the Archbishop confided to them the Church of St. James on Aisquith and Eager Streets. This was a church for the English-speaking that was given up to make way for the larger, St. Vincent's. This remained a Redemptorist church. It was here that they lived until the rectory at St. Alphonsus' was completed. See Wuest, *Annales*, vol. 1, pp. 74-85, 113-115; Byrne, *Redemptorist Centenaries*, pp. 93-96; RABB, *The Province Story,* vol. 1 (May 1, 1975), pp. 1-4.

166. After he had settled his personal and family affairs and conducted business in Europe for the Redemptorist, Fr. Benedict Bayer joined them and was professed at St. James on

July 2, 1842. His brother Joseph also joined the Congregation and was professed as Brother Gabriel Bayer on July 3, 1847. See Wuest, *Annales*, vol. 1, pp. 121-122, 454, 459. See also B. Bayer, "Relatio" in Wuest, *Annales, Supplementum,* Pt. 1, pp. 336-358.

167. One notes that Fey is now Father Fey. He was ordained by Archbishop Eccleston on June 5, 1841. The first Redemptorist ordained in the United States, he was the first and the last to say his "First Mass" at St. John's. He came to America with Father Alexander in March, 1841, as a seminarian. See Curley, *Provincial Story*, p. 363; RABB, *The Province Story,* vol. 1 (May 1, 1975), p. 14.

168. Neumann is the first Redemptorist professed in the United States. See Berger, *Life*, pp. 251-252; Curley, *Neumann*, p. 92. For his happiness as a Redemptorist, see the letter to his parents of Oct. 12, 1842, Baltimore, RABB, N., RP. Writing of this event in 1888, Wuest remarks: "Sent here and there by reason of the times to help the other priests in the sacred ministry, [Neumann] learned the religious life not from books and instructions, but from all kinds of hardships and very severe trials and in such a way that he later became a model and teacher of many." See *Annales*, vol. 1, p. 121.

169. In a little over one typed page, Neumann covers ten years of his life. Readers, desirous of more, will have to stay close to the Neumann literature. From his letters one can see his joy in his pastoral life, in enkindling fervor by the Eucharist and confraternities. One can read of his insistence on the need of priests who can minister to the Germans and keep their faith and practice alive, and prevent them from being misled by proselytizing groups and Secret Societies. See RABB, N., RP, Neumann to his parents, Oct. 12, 1842, Baltimore; Neumann to the Archbishop of Vienna, Dec. 6, 1842, Baltimore, in *Berichte,* Heft 17 (1843), pp. 43-52. See similar sentiments in an earlier letter of May 4, 1841, in *Berichte,* Heft 15 (1842), pp. 56-62.

170. From April 17 to July 17, Canon Joseph Salzbacher was sent by the Leopoldine Society to visit the Church in the United States. The money sent from the Mission Societies in Europe was sent to the American bishops. The German immigrants here sent back complaints of discrimination and of not receiving their share. More than one bishop was incensed by an investigation by a foreigner. The Canon wrote a very informative account of his visit. See T. Roemer, O.F.M. Cap., *The Ludwig-Mission-Verein and the Church in the United States* (Washington, D.C., 1933), pp. 17-19, 42-43. See also *Catholic Historical Review,* vol. 1 (1914-15), pp. 357-358.

171. Wuest remarks that Neumann did most of this work because he was well versed in making the rounds of mission stations. Cumberland and Frederick are in Maryland; York, Columbia and Strassburg (Shrewsbury) are in Pennsylvania. Not only Richmond, but Harpers Ferry and Martinsburg were then in Virginia. Since 1863 the last two are in West Virginia. The direction and mileage from Baltimore are given in parentheses: Cumberland (180 W by N.), Harpers Ferry (80 W), Martinsburg (100 W), Frederick (60 W), Richmond (146 S), Columbia (71 N), York (57 N), Strassburg-Shrewsbury (40 N). See Wuest, *Annales*, vol. 1, pp. 123-124, n. 2. To appreciate these distances, see the composite map of these states in *National Geographic Atlas of the World* (1975), 29-31. To identify these places on individual maps of Pennsylvania, Maryland, Virginia and West Virginia, see *Rand McNally Road Atlas* (51 ed. Chicago, 1975), 48-49, 88-89, 96-97.

172. Beck, *Goldenes Jubiläum,* p. 141.

173. The financial problems in building St. Philomena's were many. Father Cartuyvel's methods antagonized some, and he was replaced by Father Fey. After a short stay Fey pleaded to be relieved of the burden. Neumann came and did the lion's share of building St. Philomena's. See Curley, *Neumann*, pp. 98-100.

174. The Cause of Father Seelos has been introduced at

Rome. See Michael J. Curley, *Cheerful Ascetic. The Life of Francis Xavier Seelos, C.SS.R.*, New Orleans, 1969.

175. The church was completed and dedicated by Bishop O'Connor on Oct. 1, 1846. See *Pittsburgh Catholic,* Oct. 10, 1846; Beck, *Goldenes Jubiläum,* pp. 159-160. So much is left out. For the spiritual build-up of the parish, Neumann and his Redemptorist community, the care of German settlements elsewhere, the giving of missions and retreats, see RABB, N., Pittsburgh Years; Berger, *Life*, pp. 260-281; Beck, *Goldenes Jubiläum,* pp. 150-164; Curley, *Neumann*, pp. 98-105.

176. Neumann worked too hard and put off seeing a doctor. When his cough and bleeding persisted, his confreres reported the condition to the American Superior, Father Czackert, who ordered Neumann to come to Baltimore. See RABB, N, Pittsburgh Years, Chackert [sic] to Joseph Müller, Jan. 19, 1847, Baltimore; Berger, *Life*, p. 281.

177. In 1841 the Congregation was divided into provinces. In 1844 the foundations in the United States were placed under the Belgian Province. See M. De Meulemeester, *Outline History of the Redemptorists* (Louvain, 1956), pp. 150-157. Father Frederick De Held, the Provincial of the Belgian Province, made a vigorous visitation of the American foundations from May to August, 1845. At the end of the visitation the Hungarian, Father Alexander Czvitkovicz, was replaced by the Bohemian, Father Peter Czackert, as Superior or Vicegerent in the United States. See Curley, *Provincial Story*, pp. 79-82.

178. Father Czackert did not completely satisfy De Held's program and he was replaced by Neumann, who ruled from 1847 to 1849 as the fifth Superior in the United States. His successor, Father Bernard Hafkenscheid, arrived here on Jan. 9, 1849. He was in office from 1849 to 1853. Under him the foundations in the United States were constituted a Province on June 29, 1850. Hafkenscheid was later the one elected to be the first Provincial and he began his term on Jan. 1, 1851. He chose Neumann to be one of his two Provincial Consultors.

Sce Curley, *Provincial Story*, pp. 93-115. For Neumann's term in office as Vicegerent and then Vice-Provincial, see Curley, *Neumann*, pp. 121-153.

179. When the American Province was canonically erected, the local Superior was called a Rector. Neumann was the first Canonical Rector at St. Alphonsus'. Neumann tells us that he was installed on April 1. Wuest (*Annales*, vol. 2, p. 153) says that he was named first Rector on Jan. 2, 1851. These are not contradictory statements. The installation took place after Hafkenscheid returned from Europe as first Provincial in March, 1851. See Curley, *Provincial Story*, pp. 113-116. As seen from Neumann's letters this was a very happy period of parochial ministry, community life, and missions. See RABB, N, RP, Neumann to his father and sisters, July 10, 1851, Baltimore; Neumann to his father and relatives, Sept. 10, 1851, Baltimore. Generous excerpts are given by Berger, *Life*, pp. 310-312. Little did he think that 1852 would see him a bishop.

180. For the documents involved in Neumann's becoming a bishop, see A. Sampers, "De eligendo beato Joanne Nep. Neumann in episcopum de Philadelphia documenta Romana (Oct. 1851—Feb. 1852)," *Spicilegium Historicum* C.SS.R., vol. 11 (1963), pp. 306-321.

181. A thorough and detailed account is found in Curley, *Neumann,* pp. 165-181.

182. This is the fifth petition of the prayer, *Anima Christi,* a prayer that was known as far back as the fourteenth century. See M. Barry, "Anima Christi," *New Catholic Encyclopedia*, vol. 1 (1967), p. 544.

Index

Alphonsis, St., regard for teaching of St. Theresa of Avila, 66; abbreviations of both saints at the beginning of the autobiography, 66.

Astronomy, N.'s interest in, 74.

Autobiography, Hafkenscheid orders N. to write, 8; description of manuscript, 8-9; edited by A. Sampers, 10; translation of, 10-12; importance of, 12-15.

Baltimore, First Plenary Council of (1852), commissions N. to write or choose a German catechism, 71.

Baraga, Frederick, apostle to the Indians, his letters to Europe inspire N.'s missionary plans, 22, 75-76.

Bayer, Rev. Benedict, C.SS.R., 34, 103, 104.

Bellarmine, St. Robert, N. studies his teachings, 78-79.

Berger, Rev. John, C.SS.R., N.'s nephew, comes to America, 69; joins the Redemptorists, 69; first biographer of N., 69.

Botany, N.'s special interest in, 74.

Bruté, Simon, Bishop of Vincennes, N. hopes to be accepted by, 25, 26, 82-83, 85-86.

Buffalo area of New York, mission stations where N. worked, 92-93.

Canisius, St. Peter, N. studies his writings, 78-79.

Neumann, Joan (later, Sister Caroline), sister of N., 16; joins the Sisters of Mercy of St. Charles Borromeo, 16, 68; N. visits her in Prague, 68; testified at Budweis Process of N.'s Cause, 68; death, 68.

Neumann, John, C.SS.R., birth and baptism, 16, 67; early home training, 17; grammar school, 17; love of reading, 17; Confession, Confirmation and First Holy Communion, 17-18; attitude toward priesthood as a child, 18; proficiency in catechism, 18; studies Latin with catechist, Father Peter Schmidt, 18; enters Budweis *Gymnasium* in 1823, 18; boarding conditions, 19; early difficulties with alcoholic teacher, 19; dissatisfied with religion teacher, 19; educational crisis of 1827, temptation to give up school, 20; returns to the study of the Humanities, 20; Philosophical Studies 1829-1831, 20-22; delighted with the Cistercian teachers, 20; attraction to natural sciences, 20; greater attraction to study medicine than theology, 20; father willing to let him study medicine at Prague, 20; mother encourages him to apply for admission to the Seminary, 21; theological studies at Budweis and Prague 1831-1835, 21; special attraction for Scripture, 21; the evolution of his missionary plans for the United States, 23-26; move to Prague Seminary in the hopes of learning more languages, 22; displeased with the theology professors and the spirit of Josephinism, 22; learns. from H. Dichtl through A. Räss that Bishop Kenrick of Philadelphia needs priests, 23; no ordination for N.'s class that year, 23; pain of telling his parents about leaving without being ordained, 24; departs from home without a formal farewell 24; travels from Budweis to Linz to Munich, 24; at Munich, learns from M. Henni that Kenrick revoked the authorization for priests, 25; Professor Phillips offers to write to Bishop Bruté, 25; travels from Munich to Augsburg and Strassburg, 25; disappointing meeting with A. Räss, 25; Räss promises to write to the bishop of New York, 25; in Paris, awaiting news from Bruté, 26; problem of lodging, 26; travel to Havre, 26; books passage on the *Europa*, 27; arrival at New York and welcomed and ordained by Dubois, 28; sets out for mission station in the Buffalo district and stops off at Rochester to minister to Germans, 28; meets Father Prost, 28; meets Father Pax in Buffalo who accompanied him to Williamsville, 28; his mission stations, 28-33; change of residence from Williamsville to North

BOOKS & MEDIA

The Daughters of St. Paul operate book and media centers at the following addresses. Visit, call or write the one nearest you today, or find us on the World Wide Web, www.pauline.org

CALIFORNIA
3908 Sepulveda Blvd., Culver City, CA 90230; 310-397-8676
5945 Balboa Ave., San Diego, CA 92111; 858-565-9181
46 Geary Street, San Francisco, CA 94108; 415-781-5180

FLORIDA
145 S.W. 107th Ave., Miami, FL 33174; 305-559-6715

HAWAII
1143 Bishop Street, Honolulu, HI 96813; 808-521-2731
Neighbor Islands call: 800-259-8463

ILLINOIS
172 North Michigan Ave., Chicago, IL 60601; 312-346-4228

LOUISIANA
4403 Veterans Memorial Blvd., Metairie, LA 70006; 504-887-7631

MASSACHUSETTS
Rte. 1, 885 Providence Hwy., Dedham, MA 02026; 781-326-5385

MISSOURI
9804 Watson Rd., St. Louis, MO 63126; 314-965-3512

NEW JERSEY
561 U.S. Route 1, Wick Plaza, Edison, NJ 08817; 732-572-1200

NEW YORK
150 East 52nd Street, New York, NY 10022; 212-754-1110
78 Fort Place, Staten Island, NY 10301; 718-447-5071

OHIO
2105 Ontario Street, Cleveland, OH 44115; 216-621-9427

PENNSYLVANIA
9171-A Roosevelt Blvd., Philadelphia, PA 19114; 215-676-9494

SOUTH CAROLINA
243 King Street, Charleston, SC 29401; 843-577-0175

TENNESSEE
4811 Poplar Ave., Memphis, TN 38117; 901-761-2987

TEXAS
114 Main Plaza, San Antonio, TX 78205; 210-224-8101

VIRGINIA
1025 King Street, Alexandria, VA 22314; 703-549-3806

CANADA
3022 Dufferin Street, Toronto, Ontario, Canada M6B 3T5; 416-781-9131
1155 Yonge Street, Toronto, Ontario, Canada M4T 1W2; 416-934-3440

¡También somos su fuente para libros, videos y música en español!